MASTERING ACCELERATED LEARNING

THE ART OF RAPID SKILL ACQUISITION, MEMORY ENHANCEMENT, AND LIGHTNING-FAST COMPREHENSION

JORDAN WILLIAMS

Independently published |

IVA Publishing, Bogdan Ivanov

Württembergische Str. 18, 10707 Berlin, Germany

ISBN: 979-8870784670 Paperback

ISBN: 979-8870784908 Hardcover

Disclaimer-Notice÷

Please note the information contained within this document is for educational and entertainment purposes only. All effort has been executed to present accurate, up to date, reliable, complete information. No warranties of any kind are declared or implied. Readers acknowledge that the author is not engaged in the rendering of legal, financial, medical or professional advice. The content within this book has been derived from various sources. Please consult a licensed professional before attempting any techniques outlined in this book.

By reading this document, the reader agrees that under no circumstances is the author responsible for any losses, direct or indirect, that are incurred as a result of the use of the information contained within this document, including, but not limited to, errors, omissions, or inaccuracies.

DEDICATION

This book is dedicated to all of you out there with a dream, a vision, and the courage to try and make it a reality. To those who believe in the power of never giving up, and in the power of transforming your life for the better. I want to express my admiration and respect for your courage, your strength, and your determination. You are embarking on an incredible journey, and I hope this book will provide you with the support, guidance, and inspiration to make your dreams come true. Thank you for having the courage to believe in yourself and to make the changes necessary to achieve your goals. I have faith that you can do it!

CONTENTS

66 Learning is the only thing the mind never
exhausts, never fears, and never regrets.

– Leonardo da Vinci

INTRODUCTION

Many things in this world arouse curiosity, many ideas are waiting to be brought to reality, and many talents leave people awestruck. People often strongly desire to learn these things, and they tell themselves, "One day, I'll also learn this." Yet that "one day" never arrives. You may have a long list of things you want to learn or do, but you keep putting them off. Take a moment to consider all these things you want to learn or achieve. What have you planned? How and when are you going to learn that? What is holding you back from starting?

You may have heard about some people who are incredibly talented and brilliant. Everyone is familiar with the name Einstein. He is regarded as the nineteenth century's genius due to his extraordinary contributions to science. Many others, such as Nikola Tesla, Charles Darwin, Leonardo da Vinci, Napoleon Bonaparte, Galileo Galilei, and many more, are renowned in their respective fields. Do you know what they all had in common? They were fast learners and had positive mindsets.

Most people believe these geniuses had God-given talent, and they believe their minds cannot function like that. We prefer not to participate in real-life competitions because we spend too much time in an inner world of imagination, desires, and obsessions. We believe that creativity and brilliance are inherent skills. We tell ourselves that we are not intelligent enough to make breakthroughs and that trying something new would be a waste of our lives. Let me tell you one thing—these assumptions are incorrect. My fundamental conviction is that human potential is one of the few untapped resources on the planet. The human mind is the ultimate superpower; there are no boundaries to our inventiveness, perseverance, or capacity for thought. Everything else is limited. However, this resource is one of the least used.

Anyone can learn as fast as these geniuses were able to learn. Anyone can make remarkable discoveries and contributions in their area of interest. Anyone can be a scientist; anyone can be a genius. All you need to do is have the proper mindset. Among all these geniuses, I am the greatest fan of Nikola Tesla. Numerous technologies that are in today's world, essential to our daily lives, were developed, predicted, or invented by Tesla. These include smartphones, remote control, wireless transmission, neon and fluorescent lighting, X-rays, computers, laser beams, robotics, and alternating current (AC)—the foundation of our modern electrical system. He devised the AC production and transmission technique and created the first AC motor. He was a great learner, and his purpose in life was clear: to make energy and technology accessible to everyone. For that, he worked and learned all his life.

When we discuss learning, we mean the process of incorporating new knowledge, concepts, and abilities into our minds. We start learning while still in the womb and keep learning throughout our lives, always trying to learn new things and improve our skill sets. Every new piece of knowledge we acquire expands what we already know and deepens our comprehension of the world. A better understanding of the world makes it easier to adjust to new circumstances and redirect our course when something unfavorable occurs.

Many people find learning challenging if they were misguided in their early years of education. Often, people are not taught how to memorize, comprehend, or learn things correctly. Instead, rote memorization and other outdated learning methods dominate their school years. Studying in school can be a torturous process for many people, who often despise learning for the rest of their lives as they equate learning with their school experiences.

However, learning is much more than simply studying like you did in school. Once you begin learning, you will notice how your entire life pattern changes. It is a growth process. It is a lifestyle. But before you start learning, you should be clear about your life goals and purpose, so your energies are spent on the right things.

Have you ever thought about your purpose in life? Most individuals have no idea what their purpose is, and don't even want to know since they are so used to going with the flow. They don't want to leave their comfort zones. If this describes you, you might ask yourself, "What's wrong with living a simple, uncomplicated life?" It's not a bad idea to live a simple life, but try to make it the best it can be by incorporating learning into your daily routine and focusing your energy in the right direction.

However, I want to say one thing here: You only live once. What's holding you back from recognizing your potential and becoming a genius when you will never have another chance at life?

From the study of biology, we know that species that are adaptable and flourish within their ever-evolving habitats are the ones that survive. Those that are unable to adapt to their surroundings ultimately go extinct. The same holds true for people in both their personal and professional lives. Maybe you are familiar with someone at work who has not adjusted their behavior in response to the rapid pace of societal change. Because they are hesitant to challenge or educate themselves on anything new, it seems they are regressing, and soon they will be left behind. People risk becoming intellectually stagnant if they won't simply absorb new ideas and information. Both participation and active participation are required for learning anything new.

What you believe you already know might be the most destructive to your personal and professional growth. Many people think there is no place for new ideas because they already know everything. They are afraid of learning because learning something new implies that they might have to change their perspective. Changing their long-established thoughts is so difficult for them that they prefer staying ignorant. Remember, you won't go far if you don't want to let go of your preconceived notions. Defeating your ego might be one of the most challenging tasks you'll face while attempting to learn anything new. Therefore, the quality that will help you learn the most is the willingness to acknowledge when you are incorrect and to make necessary adjustments to your thinking. Admitting your ignorance and deciding to act are the first steps in learning.

Many people believe that there is nothing special in their lives, and they are born to be ordinary. What if you are an average person with nothing remarkable to give as a purpose in life? Well, I have to disagree with this idea that you have absolutely nothing to offer. I believe you haven't yet found your true self, and are unaware of your hidden abilities. In this book, we will talk about how the human brain is limitless and how everyone has something remarkable to contribute— you just haven't realized it yet. This book explains how to discover your life's purpose and hidden abilities. Once you find out your hidden talent, you can use it to your advantage and to benefit humanity.

You will learn in this book how much potential is hidden inside you that you need to explore. The only problem with us is that we settle for what we think we are; we don't consider ourselves capable of doing great things. By constantly telling ourselves that we are ordinary, we end up becoming ordinary. This book aims to help you understand that you are a unique species that has evolved to rule this planet, and that you are not ordinary.

There is another reason we are not very good at learning. The contemporary environment trains us to be in a continuous state of preoccupation and makes it difficult to pay attention. It is tempting to check your phone every few seconds for the newest notification, but to learn, your whole attention must be on the task at hand. When you are in a situation in which you are distracted, further information cannot establish itself in your consciousness. As a result, you end up with knowledge gaps.

The ability to focus is a skill that can be developed, through practice and ingenuity, into structures that enable you to offer your undivided attention to whatever it is that you are studying.

If you had the ability to learn quicklier, more wisely, and more effectively, you could apply it to whatever subject you wanted to pursue. These strategies could be used for anything, from learning Spanish to mastering your willpower or mentality. There is no limit to what you could do with these techniques. Because you would no longer have any boundaries, anything at all could be accomplished. At least up to this point, the belief that you are constrained may be one thing that has prevented you from realizing your wildest goals. I assure you, though, that not one of your convictions in any way limits who you are as a person. Unleashing the boundless potential that lies dormant inside you—unrealized levels of power, intellect, and concentration—is essential to unleashing these latent abilities.

These chapters will provide you with several tools that will enable you to overcome your apparent limitations. You are going to discover how to expand your mind. You will discover how to unleash your drive. You will find ways to boost your capacity for memory, focus, and habits. This book is your road map to mastering your mind, motivation, and strategies for learning how to learn, and I am your mentor on your hero's journey. And once you have accomplished that, your options are endless. This book aims to assist you in understanding that it does not matter where you are or where you have been. You can liberate yourself and move from a place of confinement to one of freedom. That might be the only "plus" you require to move from the ordinary world to the extraordinary one.

To master any new skill as rapidly as possible, I embarked on a personal journey to test the art and science of rapid skill acquisition. This book aims to speed up learning new abilities for you. It outlines a systematic strategy for learning new abilities as rapidly as possible. These methods are applicable everywhere, for any skill you want to learn. It doesn't matter if you want to create a business, publish a book, paint a portrait, learn a new language, or simply manage your home in your daily routine. You will be astonished at how excellent you'll become if you devote just a few hours to learning the fundamentals of the skill. This book will enable you to learn any skill you desire in less time and with less wasted effort. You may immediately increase your performance with a little concentrated, planned action.

Learning entails setting aside time for reflective thinking. It calls for contemplating what you have learned and allowing your thoughts to roam freely. You have to let go of the idea that you need to seem intelligent, and instead concentrate on really being intelligent. Often, we have difficulty learning because we have unrealistic expectations about how simple it should be. The difficulty level of each skill varies, which is why it is better to understand which skill you will learn and which is best suited for you right now. This book will guide you step by step on how you can choose a task, how you can start working on it, and which areas of the new skill should be focused on first. Set small goals for yourself in each learning process. Every little accomplished goal will give you a sense of achievement and confidence in yourself and help you move forward.

Another thing that is very closely associated with learning is memory. Without memory, learning is impossible.

Anything you "know" must be securely stored in your memory to be considered "learned." What good is it to learn something more quickly if you soon forget it? It is crucial to initially improve memory capacity if you want to retain information for a more extended period. Simply learning something is not enough; you also need to remember it.

Information acquisition, storage, retention, and subsequent retrieval are all psychological processes referred to as *memory*. The capacity of human memory includes the ability to store and retrieve data. This method is not perfect, though. People occasionally fail to remember, or they make errors. Sometimes, information is not properly stored in memory.

The information must be converted into a usable format to build a new memory, accomplished through encoding. The information must be kept in memory for future use after it has been successfully encoded. For this reason, studying and practicing material helps with memory. The neurons that store that memory become more connected with practice. The data encoded into memory must first be recovered to be used.

The kind of information being used and the presence of retrieval signals are just two of the numerous variables that may impact this process. We can truly use our long-term memories to make decisions, communicate with others, and solve problems since we can access and recover information from them. But memories need to be structured in some form to be retrievable.

In some cases, specific triggers might work as potent triggers to bring memories back into the present moment. One example is smell. A rush of vivid memories associated with people and events from someone's past can come rushing back when they smell a fragrance. In this book, we will talk about how the senses of smell, taste, and sight are very helpful for memorization. Your brain makes memories in the form of images. Thus, visuals also enhance your learning experience. Other things that affect memory are a healthy lifestyle, regular exercise, and a healthy diet. These things can also help to increase memory capacity.

Different forms of creativity can also stimulate the brain and speed up learning and memory. Sleeping enough is also essential for healthy brain function. Chunking the primary data is an additional method for enhancing memory and learning capacity. In short, whatever your current level of memory proficiency, there are certainly a few things you can do to improve it. We will talk about how to study and learn more effectively so that you may learn more in less time, as well as the role of recalling information and teaching others to enhance your memory. There are a ton of fun new techniques to strengthen your memory. Be patient while reading this book. All these details will be revealed to you gradually.

Because you are reading this book, you are far ahead of most people who merely accept their current circumstances and restrictions. You are a member of a select group of people who are prepared to go the extra mile to achieve their goals in life. In other words, you've embraced the call of adventure. It doesn't matter how much information you have if you can't properly use it to benefit yourself. As a result, the helpful inputs you accumulate while reading this book must be transformed into sound output. To expose and fulfill our full potential while motivating others to do the same is, in my opinion, the ultimate journey we are all on.

CHAPTER 1
THE OCEAN OF KNOWLEDGE

" The illiterate of the 21st century will not be those who cannot read and write, but those who cannot learn, unlearn, and relearn.

ALVIN TOFFLER

I n the last few decades, there has been an explosion in the world of knowledge, with millions and billions of books published yearly. The usage of print and electronic media is expanding at an accelerated rate. This sudden surge in knowledge supply is known as an information explosion. It can be said that the observation of the excessive expansion of information, in comparison to other facets of the social or economic order, is also an information explosion. This explosion, however, focuses more on the quantity of newly produced information than its quality.

When a person is exposed to an ocean of information, using the right information filters or sorting choices to find the right materials is more problematic than simply having the information or expertise available. Finding accurate and crucial information is therefore challenging due to information overload. According to several calculations, scientific knowledge doubles every 100 years. Recent estimates say that the world's knowledge is doubling, on average, every five to twelve years, and this rate is rapidly increasing.

Information is growing quickly in many industries, including government, commerce, and healthcare. Journalism is another industry that is being impacted by this phenomenon. The abundance of knowledge in today's world may suffocate a profession that was in charge of disseminating information in the past. Previously, people relied on *CNN*, the *New York Times*, and other mainstream media organizations for accurate information. Nowadays, most of the information people consume comes from social media, blogs, articles, and YouTube. Although people know that this information might not be correct, they still rely on these mediums because of the more interesting way the news is presented.

The rate of information production and consumption steadily increases for a good reason. Education and information become more easily accessible and cheaper, which results in a more educated public. This in turn allows for an increase in the number of people who could add to the available knowledge. Everyone starts contributing in their own way. Just as the sea level rises every year, similarly, this ocean of knowledge is also expanding every year. But this explosion of knowledge, although advantageous at many levels, is also producing problems.

Filtering the data is also getting tougher than before. "Filtering" refers to finding valuable information related to data scientists' work within a sea of data. Another point to consider is the legal and ethical guidelines, which relate to who will be the data owner, how frequently they are obliged to release this and for how long, who can have access to that data, and who can legally manipulate it.

This data explosion hasn't stopped there. Indeed, it has expanded in every possible direction of available knowledge. It's clear why. Anyone, anywhere, may innovate and add to the ocean of knowledge, since people have access to enormous amounts of information and technology.

SKILLS THAT MATTER

Being surrounded by ever-expanding information makes it impossible to stay updated on everything in every field of knowledge. Even keeping yourself updated in one particular field is equally as impossible. Suppose I am a physics student doing research in the nanotechnology field. It's not possible for me to research all the areas of physics. I might still miss information, and even if I spend all day and all night with knowledge resources, I cannot absorb everything related to

3

my field. So what is the purpose of all this information, and what can we do while stuck in this era?

According to *Future Shock* author Alvin Toffler, "The illiterate of the 21st century will not be those who cannot read and write, but those who cannot learn, unlearn and relearn." Therefore, acquiring every piece of knowledge in this universe is not the objective. But to keep ourselves open to learning and to unlearn according to the consequences. As a person living in the twenty-first century, you need to manage social interactions successfully, get along with technology, stay current on politics, follow the law, handle your finances, keep yourself open to learning and unlearning, and make wise job selections.

Every additional life skill you need can be unlocked through learning. People build these talents over their first twenty to twenty-five years of life, from kindergarten through graduate school, including reading, general knowledge, analytical and critical thinking, and ultimately innovative thinking. This makes "effective learning" the sole skill that truly matters, because once you master it, you can learn basically any other skill. In all their years of formal education, most people were not taught how to learn. They were just presented with a bunch of information, and then they were assessed on that, but what about the actual learning skill? Why are people never taught this basic skill? Why don't people know how to make the best of their brains while learning?

Let's pause for a moment to appreciate how remarkable your brain is. A brain can process a plethora of information and thoughts each day. It has infinite storage capacity and amazing analysis skills, yet every brain differs from others.

Look around you and see the cars people are driving, the technology people are using, the essential elements in daily life, the rockets that are sent into space, and the many other uncountable inventions by the human brain. Isn't it fascinating? It's just another person's brain, like yours, that imagined something and brought it to reality. This is the power of the human brain, and these are only a few examples of a human brain's capability. In reality, the human brain is limitless.

Have you ever thought about why people are Earth's most dominant and powerful species? If you assess yourself physically, you'll find that you're just average. Many other animals are stronger than humans. They can run much faster, have sharper vision, fly in the air, and breathe underwater. But humans are the rulers of Earth. It is simply because of their brains. People's bodies might not be as strong physically, but they have developed instruments that make them much stronger. People's eyesight is just average, but with their brains, people have developed technologies that can help them see the galaxy they are part of, and beyond.

I cannot jot down all the wonders of the human brain here, because it's impossible. But mentioning these inventions will give you the idea that a normal human brain can do wonders, because it is superior to all other creatures.

People used to believe that their brains experienced their neurological peak in late adolescence, and after that, they did nothing but decay. But this is not the case. Human brains are capable of neuroplasticity, meaning that people's behaviors and surroundings may alter and shape their brains. Your brain is always changing to accommodate your environment and your desires. So the brain should never be underestimated; it evolves with the changing environment and other conditions. The brain of a person born in poverty might function differently than the brain of a person brought up in a luxurious environment.

A person who faces difficult circumstances develops their brain so that working hard is a part of their routine, and their thoughts circulate around bread and butter. In contrast, the ones who haven't faced any hardships cannot work like those born in such undesirable conditions. So the brain of both these people will function differently; their preferences will be different, and their life choices will be different. Each of these brains has learned everything according to their capacities and the environment in which they are living.

To enhance our learning process, first, we need to understand the senses that help us learn. The major role in our learning and memory is played by the sense of smell and sense of taste. When you talk about delicious food, why do you feel your mouth getting watery? Because you just remembered the food's taste and smell. Even if the food is not in front of you, you can still vividly imagine it.

Similarly, many events in your life may be associated with different fragrances: the smell of rain, the smell of the food cooked by your parents, the perfume that your favorite teacher wore, and so on. If you ever catch up with such a fragrance, it will take you back to the days when you made memories with that smell.

That's how strong these senses are. It is often suggested to relate a memory with a certain fragrance so that it stays vivid in your brain. Another amazing sense that helps in the learning process is the visual sense. As *Homo sapiens*, we have a remarkable aptitude for learning through vivid, visual, and hands-on experiences. Think about cavemen; they didn't know how to read and write. How did they communicate and remember things at that time? They drew paintings on the walls, which helped them remember things and learn. Also, these cavemen used a sense of smell and a sense of taste to understand the right places to get food and where they would encounter a poisonous herb. The visuals and drawings then helped them pass their knowledge to others.

HOW TO USE SKILL TREES TO BUILD NEW SKILLS

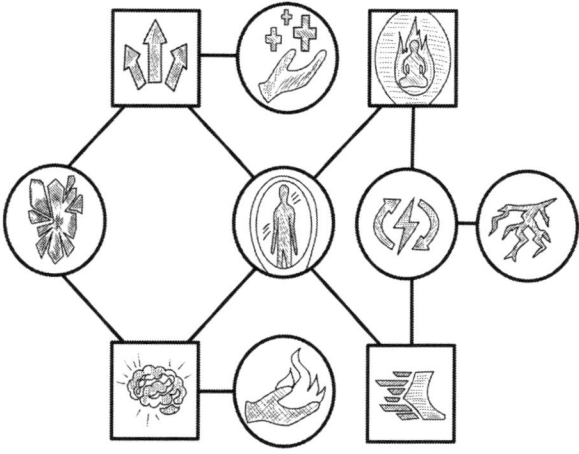

A skill tree is a graphic representation of the minor skills needed to learn more complex abilities. Skill trees are borrowed from video games like *Diablo* and *World of Warcraft*. In these games, each character has a specific skill tree, which helps the player decide which path is more suitable to take to progress efficiently.

Similarly, in *Dota 2*, there is a talent tree for heroes that allows them to unlock new abilities as their levels increase. In these games, lower-tier skills that are acquired in the earlier levels allow players to become more trained in complex skills later in the game.

In the same way, if you find learning challenging and cannot decide what to learn now or in the future, then the skill tree might help you. Skill trees will help you develop focus, guide your learning process, and make it easy to assess the progress of your learning goals. You can easily learn and understand other connected skills by learning some smart skills first. The skill tree can be used to map the learning objective and make decisions about whether to move forward with the subject matter.

Skill trees increase your self-awareness by forcing you to delve deep into the subskills you have mastered and those you need to learn. You will chart out all the necessary subskills when you create your skill tree, along with your current competence level in each one. Make a note of the various resources you believe could aid you in learning from the results. Ask specialists about the talents you want to learn if you have access to them. Once you have organized everything and assessed your proficiency in each subskill, you can begin to channel your focus. You may begin planning and carrying out activities after knowing where to direct your attention.

STEPS FOR BUILDING A SKILL TREE

To maximize your learning experience, follow these steps when building a skill tree. These are not hard and fast rules, but they can give you an idea of how you can build your skill tree.

1. Identify the skill you want to learn: This is the most crucial step, as you need to understand which skills are suitable for you and practically beneficial. People often waste their time learning a skill unrelated to their work, so it's important to wisely decide where it's worth investing your time.

2. List the principles, details, and steps: For inspiration, search the Internet to see how people are acquiring the particular skill you have decided to learn. Ask people around you who are proficient in that skill. Search as much as you can, and then make bullet points for yourself. Jot down anything that needs to be understood, memorized, and practiced, and think as deeply as possible.

3. Build the skill tree: Break down your skill into further subskills, and build a tree to guide you on which subskills you need to master before moving on to the main skill you want to learn. Assign the required time to each subskill. Make sure that these subskills will contribute to your efforts in learning the main skill, and your efforts will not be in vain. Highlight the areas you want to direct your focus. Highlighting will assist you in focusing your attention, studying the proper material, and keeping you informed of any additional material you may need to learn in the future or have previously studied. Draw and redraw until it is the best you can make for yourself.

4. Self-assess: Once you start learning the subskills, rate yourself periodically. It will help you assess where you stand in your learning and identify whether your pace is well suited to your targeted goal or not. It is better to rate yourself before learning the skill and then rate your performance after learning it. You can also ask your friends, family, or coworkers, to rate your performance.

These steps can be altered slightly according to your requirements, but this skill tree will definitely help you to learn faster and more effectively.

HOW AN ADULT BRAIN ABSORBS KNOWLEDGE

Learning in adults can have a very positive effect on their lives. By learning a certain skill, they can boost their earnings and contribute more to the region's economy, especially in developing countries that are already struggling against poverty. Adult learning can also positively influence their social interactions and family relationships. Claims that the human brain starts to deteriorate after a certain age are outdated. This does not happen unless a person is suffering from a serious brain disease or other health condition. The human mind is always open to learning.

The brain's capacity to change and adapt due to experience is known as *neuroplasticity*. It also goes by the name *brain plasticity*. The term *plasticity* describes the brain's malleability, characterized as being "easily affected, trained, or controlled." Neuroplasticity helps people learn things, adapt to any environment, and enhance cognitive functions. The brain's malleability is so amazing that it even helps many people recover from brain injuries or strokes.

How an adult's brain learns something new differs greatly from how a child's brain learns something new. Adult learners are rarely motivated to learn just because someone else says so. Adults enter the learning environment with deeply held ideas about how things function. They have a better time processing the world around them and building strong connections between their memories. In light of their experiences, they question things around them.

People will ask themselves, "Why do I need to learn this? What impact will it have on my life? How can I contribute to it? And what are its similarities and differences to what I have learned before?" But when someone studies something entirely unfamiliar to them, they don't question it, because they don't have any prior knowledge to relate to it or to judge it by. Because they are open to receiving what is being taught to them, they will suddenly improve as learners.

This is why it is often advised to learn as a child. Once you have decided to learn something, learn as if you know nothing, and don't judge anything based on your prior knowledge. This will help you learn better.

Readiness to absorb knowledge can also make you a better learner. As adult learners, people usually look for the outcomes of that learning process. It is better to integrate what you have learned into your life. Once your brain observes the application of what it is learning, it will help you stay interested in learning. As adults, people become more practical; while learning something, start by presenting yourself with a problem, and then move toward its solution. This problem-solving technique enhances learning in adults.

Adults also rely on the concepts developed while learning something, which is perfectly fine. It is better to make your concepts in learning to grasp things better and stay motivated than to lose all motivation. There is a huge role of internal motivation in learning any skill. Go deep into your "why," if you want to increase your motivation to study something. Perform easy concentrating practices before and during the toughest learning moments. You will discover that it is an effective method for motivating yourself.

WHY YOU NEED TO PLAN YOUR LEARNING

A learning plan is a roadmap for individuals to direct their learning and growth. It includes a target and the precise training procedures required to achieve it. By using an effective learning plan, better goals may be defined, and specifying the necessary actions increases a learner's likelihood of achieving these goals. Setting a learning goal is very important in learning anything. It is also necessary to understand that setting these goals is not always easy. Some people clearly know what they want to accomplish at work, while others don't. So it is better to first identify why you came here. More importantly, it will offer you a sense of direction, keeping you inspired until the very end.

Here is a list of some practical steps to plan the learning procedure for any skill acquisition.

APPLY A GROWTH MENTALITY

Always open your mind when learning anything new. With a positive attitude, you will respond to setbacks or problems with optimism and confidence. Some people limit themselves by thinking that they were born with a certain skill, and it is not possible for them to learn something completely different. As we have already discussed, the plasticity of the human brain grants it the ability to learn anything. Only inner motivation is needed for that. To grow in a better way, devise a self-assessment plan for the analyses of your past and present skills and what skills you will need to learn in the future.

SET LEARNING GOALS

It is often advised to devise a personal learning plan while trying to learn anything. By making a personal learning plan, you can clearly set your goals and prioritize them. It can be beneficial to divide your long-term goal into smaller stages.

PRACTICE HARD

Once everything falls into place, it will be time to practice the skill. Practice hard and give all your efforts to learn that skill. Perfection comes with practice. Keep practicing, until you feel that you have mastered that skill.

OVERCOME BARRIERS

You will face many problems during the learning process. But once you have stepped into the learning process, make yourself strong, face every obstacle, and keep motivating yourself. Remember that consistency is the key to learning anything, so keep yourself motivated and consistent in practicing and overcoming all the barriers in your way to master the skill you are working for.

ABSORB 10 TIMES YOUR CAPACITY

Without memory, learning is impossible. You can only learn something if it is safely retained in your memory. What use is it to learn faster if you'll soon forget everything you learned? There is a great need to improve memory capacity before learning anything, so you can retain it. Memory can be improved by the practice of memorizing different things, like phone numbers, and then asking yourself if you still remember them after a while. This seems like rote memorization, but it does help to improve memory. There are a few more ways to increase your learning capacity.

We have previously discussed that sense of smell, taste, and vision help with memory. If it is impossible to associate any memory with smell or taste, you can still visualize things in your mind. The more specific the visuals, the more your brain will learn from them.

It is always a good idea to develop the visuals in your mind with things you already have some knowledge of. Your brain pays special attention to the things connected with preexisting knowledge; that's how you can make logical connections of the things you are trying to remember. It is necessary to choose the right markers that will plainly represent the details you want to recall.

Along with these ideas, other healthy activities in lifestyle can play a role in improving learning capacity. Regular exercise every week and healthy food choices make your brain strong and more open to learning. Creative activities, like painting, coloring, designing, and making DIY projects, can also help the brain become more active and learn faster. Getting enough sleep is also necessary for proper brain functioning. Get adequate amounts of sleep at night, and take power naps during the day whenever needed.

Another technique for improving memory and learning capacity is chunking the main data. You probably already use this technique. The chunking technique entails structuring the pieces after grouping them and looking for patterns. Chunking works because the mind is designed to seek patterns and connect the dots. With such sophisticated techniques to extract valuable structures from raw data, your memory system will become considerably more efficient and intelligent than it already is.

Meditation also helps to enhance working memory. Your brain ceases actively processing information when you are in a state of meditation. Take a break every now and then to clear your thoughts. You could remember a little bit more with this technique and reduce your stress level.

RETAIN KNOWLEDGE

Only learning something is not enough. You must also retain that knowledge. Since learning is a process that takes time, people cannot invest their time, again and again, into learning that skill. So it is better to make some strategies with which you can learn faster and retain the learned knowledge.

LEARN IN DIFFERENT WAYS

Instead of using one approach to learning, try different ways. For example, if you are learning something by reading a book, try watching a video on that topic. If it applies to daily life, try practicing it to learn it in a better way. Your memory is strengthened even more when you acquire knowledge in multiple ways.

TEACH SOMEONE ELSE

Whether it's just a concept or a practicing skill, teaching someone else greatly impacts knowledge retention. If you cannot readily describe an idea to someone else, you have not grasped it well enough. Teaching someone else makes you retain 90 percent of the knowledge you were learning.

STUDY SMARTER, NOT HARDER

Focus on those areas that help you learn a particular thing, instead of wasting your energy on something that doesn't matter. Another way to study smartly is to identify your potential. Which time of the day is more suitable for you, when you can build your focus in a better way? Try studying during those hours of the day. It will assist you in learning more quickly and remembering what you have already learned.

FOCUS ON ONE THING AT A TIME

Chunking the information into bits and then consuming it helps you learn better instead of consuming all the information simultaneously. So it is better to focus on one thing, and once you are confident, move forward.

GET BETTER AT TAKING NOTES

Reading and writing involve separate brain regions. If you took the time to write something down, this means that you should go over your notes again during or after reviewing the material. Note-taking is a great way to help you retain knowledge. Try making bullet points of everything you learn, and then later, by just going through those bullet points, you will immediately remember everything related to it.

GAIN PRACTICAL EXPERIENCE

Apply what you have learned in your practical life. One of the finest methods to enhance learning is to put new information and abilities into practice.

AVOID DISTRACTIONS

Distractions can largely affect your learning and retaining capabilities. One of the biggest obstacles to maintaining attention when studying is texting, social media, calls, and other technological distractions. So it's best to put your phone away while learning.

CHAPTER 2
FINDING YOUR LIFE'S CALLING

" A moment's insight is sometimes worth a life's experience

OLIVER WENDELL HOLMES

Everyone is born with an innate desire to become something in their life. It's referred to as our life's task. This goal is quite clear at a young age, but as you grow, the pressure of family and society can mold your thoughts into becoming something they want instead. This creates a gap in your personality and contributes to distress among many young people. It is never too late to respond to your inner calling and work toward what you truly want in life. Once you direct all your focus and energies to something you desire, you will accomplish it. But first, you need to identify that inner voice.

If you haven't given much thought to your purpose in life, you may have preconceived notions about life's purpose.

People's upbringing will frequently shape these notions about life in their families and communities. Their lives are often about getting married and raising children. Or perhaps it's about obtaining a certain financial goal or position in society. A happy family, a fulfilling career, and a robust social network may seem like the formula for the ideal life. However, these kinds of successes often don't result in the fulfillment of discovering your unique sense of purpose. Your "why" is your purpose.

Feelings of purpose seem to have developed in humans so that people can do great things together, which may explain why it is linked to improved physical and mental health. Since it relates to evolution, the purpose is adaptive. It promotes the survival of both individuals and the species. Many believe that their unique talents and abilities to stand out from the crowd give them a sense of purpose, but that is only partially true. A person's purpose in life also develops due to their relationships with others. Upon choosing your route, you will certainly come across other people following it to reach the same goal.

Everyone has a purpose. I believe you have one. It seems clear and rational that you must be able to offer something of value that no one else can give, and that no one else on Earth is precisely like you or has the exact blend of nature and nurture. Your life's mission is that special quality; it is the gift you alone can give the world and is closely intertwined with your identity.

DISCOVER YOUR HIDDEN TALENT

Finding your hidden skills can be a very challenging task. After years of formal education, many people believe that this is what they were meant to do, even if they don't enjoy it. People think they are aware of their upside and downside. The fact is that everyone possesses undiscovered talents and abilities. To put it another way, people don't always know what they are. You can access what might be a fantastic resource to assist you in several facets of your life, if you can identify your dormant talents. A genius attempts to hit the target with all their heart, soul, and natural talent. Success always comes after the effort and skill you put into your work.

Interpersonal communication techniques are the best way to uncover hidden talent. Your talent and passion can be nailed down by asking yourself what makes you feel better, what genuinely thrills you, and why you want to undertake certain tasks. Once you have nailed it, keep working at it. Success will reward your perseverance. Your understanding of yourself is really complicated. You might be blind to what you are excellent at. Finding your most talented qualities can be challenging because they frequently appear in unexpected areas. You might even excel in areas that you consider to be your weaknesses. There are many wonderful reasons to desire to discover your talents, but it requires some effort.

Everyone is distinct from birth. Their DNA carries a genetic marker for this individuality. People are a once-in-a-lifetime phenomena in the cosmos due to their unique genetic composition, which has never occurred before and cannot be replicated. Some people experience this basic individuality more strongly than others, but it naturally wants to be known and expressed. Many of the greatest masters in history have acknowledged that they have been led onward by some type of force, voice, or feeling of destiny. We may detect this hint when we behave by following our deepest desires. We may feel that the words we speak or our physical gestures come to us so quickly and naturally that they originate elsewhere.

Your level of submission to different forces in life and society's demands is what lessens this power. It causes you not to experience it or even doubt its existence. This counterforce is capable of great potency. You want to blend in with the crowd. You might unconsciously feel uncomfortable or embarrassed by what makes you unique. Your parents might also serve as a counterforce. They might try to steer you toward a wealthy and satisfying profession. If these counterforces become too powerful, you risk losing any sense of your individuality and who you truly are. Your preferences and desires start to take after those of others.

You might go down a very dangerous path if you do this.

You ultimately settle on a profession that isn't a good fit for you. Your motivation and attention gradually diminish, and your job suffers as a result. You start to realize that happiness and contentment are things that come from sources other than your job. Because you are becoming less committed to your profession, you cannot recognize changes in the sector. As a result, you fall behind the times and must pay the price. Because you lack an inner sense of direction or radar to guide you, you struggle or do as others do when faced with critical decisions. You no longer have a connection to your birthright destiny. All this time, the voice inside you keeps calling you at different times. That calling is from deep within. It comes from your uniqueness. It reveals the activities that go well with your personality. And at some point, it compels you to pursue a specific line of employment or career.

People are moving into a time when their abilities to rely on the government, businesses, loved ones, and friends for support and safety is diminishing. It is a highly competitive, globalized environment, and people must learn how to improve themselves. At the same time, it is a world packed with important issues and possibilities that are best solved and exploited by entrepreneurs—individuals or small groups that think independently, react rapidly, and have distinct viewpoints. Your distinctive and creative abilities will be in high demand. Here are a few quick and easy strategies to uncover your hidden talents.

CONSIDER WHAT YOU ENJOY

Identify your hobbies and interests. Look deep into yourself and identify what you would like to do when you are free. It could be your hidden skill, if you find yourself drawn to it and can do it effortlessly with perfection. You can identify your hidden talent by engaging in self-reflective activities, letting your mind do whatever it wants, and wandering where it feels happy because these small pleasures can draw out your strengths.

ASK PEOPLE AROUND YOU

It is always a good idea to get reviews from the people around you on what they think you are good at. It is often impossible to identify things about yourself, but the people with whom you spend most of your time might make better observations of you. Ask the people you trust the most to give you their honest reviews and opinions. The people closest to you, your family, friends, and coworkers, will be able to identify some of your abilities, even when you are unable to do so.

PUSH YOURSELF TO YOUR LIMITS

People often don't want to go outside of their comfort zone, but staying in one place never allows them to find their true potential. Moreover, it makes them unproductive and stagnant. You must step outside your comfort zone to find your life's purpose, discover your strengths, and develop your abilities. You need to let go of your comfort and push yourself to the limits, where you can finally get what you were looking for.

DESCRIBE YOUR STRONG AND WEAK POINTS

Outline your strengths and weaknesses by sitting down, grabbing a pen and a piece of paper, and writing objectively about your strengths and weaknesses. Writing down your strengths and weaknesses will allow you to assess where you stand and your interests. Some people are unable to see their talents, but with a little perseverance, reflection, and focus, you can discover your talents.

INVEST IN YOUR TALENT

Just finding your talent is not enough. Talent only means that you have the potential to do something, but it doesn't guarantee any success unless you invest your time and money in it. It is always better to first identify your talent, and then invest in it in an honest way. Invest in positive courses, which will help you to polish your skill. Assign daily hours to learn that talent, so that you can excel in it.

DO NOT COPY OTHERS

Imitating others is never a solution. In today's ever-accelerating world, everyone craves newness and uniqueness. People often see that the people who come up with innovative ideas always get attention and ultimately succeed. Therefore, there is no need to copy anyone. Instead, create the ideas that naturally come to your mind. Your talent is something you were born with. You never noticed it, but it was always by your side. You don't need to copy others to excel with your talent. Listen to your inner voice; it will direct you to the path that is made for you. Be innovative and unique, instead of just following the path set by others.

STRATEGIES TO FIND YOUR CALLING

Properly finding life's task demands a lot of planning and strategizing, since there will be many difficulties on this path. The following techniques will help you overcome the five major barriers that will stand in your way: becoming infected by other people's voices, competing for scarce resources, taking the wrong turns, being trapped in the past, and losing your direction. Pay attention to them because you will almost certainly run into one of them at some point in your life.

RETURN TO YOUR ORIGINS—PRIMARY INCLINATION STRATEGY

For most people, their purpose in life lies somewhere in their childhood. You are drawn to your purpose at birth. You can feel the calling in your early years. But with passing years, that calling is suppressed due to peer and societal pressure. Sometimes, formal education becomes so tough for you to manage that you don't even have time to think about your life's purpose; thus, your natural calling fades.

The primal inclination strategy suggests returning to your origin, the days of your childhood, and the days of purity. Which thing attracted you the most at that time? What did you enjoy most in your early years? Why did you give up on it? Does it still fascinate you? For masters, their aptitude frequently manifests itself with extraordinary clarity when they are young.

A simple object may occasionally be what causes a strong response and sense of familiarity. You need to be aware of the fact that you need to engage deeply with a subject to master it. Your passion must extend beyond the subject matter, and be almost at the religious level. Putting these childlike attractions into words, which are more like sensations, profound wonder, sensual pleasure, and increased awareness, is challenging. The significance of identifying these preverbal tendencies is that they are evident signs of an attraction that is uncontaminated by other people's influences. They are not ingrained in you by your parents; rather, they have a more verbal and conscious nature and are connected to you on a more surface level. They can only be your own reflections of your chemistry, coming from a deeper source.

You frequently lose contact with these signals from your primitive core as you grow more intelligent. They might be lost among all the other topics you have studied. Reestablishing contact with this core, and returning to your roots, can determine your power and future. You must look for indications of these tendencies in your earliest years. Look for their remnants: intense emotions about something straightforward, a desire to repeat an activity you never got tired of, a topic that sparked an unusual curiosity, and feelings of power associated with specific activities. Your purpose is already present within you. You simply need to dig and unearth what has been hidden within you the entire time. There is nothing you need to build. Any time you connect with this core, a piece of that primal attraction will return to life and point you toward what may ultimately become your life's purpose.

OCCUPY YOUR NICHE—DARWINIAN STRATEGY

Some people work in industries where they must compete for resources and survival, much like an ecological system. It is more difficult to thrive in an area where many individuals are already working. Working in such an area will exhaust you as you fight for attention, play political games, and gain access to limited resources. You will spend a lot of time on things that make you tired, leaving little time for your interests and expertise. You might be drawn to these professions because you observe others making a living and following the same route, but have no idea how challenging such a life may be.

Because the game you wish to play is unique, find a niche in the surroundings that you can master. Finding such a niche is seldom an easy process. It calls for persistence and a certain approach. Start by selecting a field that approximately reflects your interests. You have two options for where to proceed from there.

The first method is to search for side pathways that appeal to you from inside your chosen field. You can go into this more specialized field and dig deeper and deeper. This procedure can be repeated until you find a completely untapped niche—the more specific, the better. This niche should somewhat reflect your individuality.

The second method is to seek out more topics or abilities you can learn once you have mastered your first one. You can now combine this additional field of knowledge with the previous one, either forming a new field or making unique links between them. You can keep going as long as you like. In the end, you will develop a field that is completely unique. This updated version fits very well with a society where access to knowledge is readily available, and sharing ideas is a source of influence.

Regardless of your selection, you will have discovered a niche that is not saturated by competition. You will be free to explore and investigate certain issues that interest you. You will control the resources available to this niche and set your own strategy. You will have the time and space to do your life's work since you won't be constrained by intense competition or political maneuvering.

AVOID FALSE PATHS—REBELLION STRATEGY

Usually, people are drawn to a false route in life for the wrong reasons, like wealth, popularity, or recognition. People frequently feel a type of emptiness when they desire attention, which they hope to fill with the illusory hive of social acceptance. People rarely get the fulfillment they want, because their career path does not align with their core motivations.

As a result, people's work degrades, and the initial attention they may have received begins to wane. When comfort and money are the deciding factors, people typically act out of worry and a desire to impress their parents and society, who may try to lead them toward something profitable out of concern. But that doesn't guarantee success and happiness.

Before your confidence suffers, you must realize as soon as possible that you made the wrong decision when choosing your career. Additionally, you should actively rebel against the forces that have steered you off your true course. Dismiss the desire for affirmation and attention because they will lead you wrong. Feel some rage toward the parental forces trying to impose a foreign career on you. Following a route separate from your parents and creating your own personality is vital to your growth. Allow your sense of disobedience to provide you with motivation and direction.

LET GO OF WHAT HAPPENED IN THE PAST —ADAPTATION STRATEGY

You shouldn't cling to old traditions, because doing so will only cause you to lag and suffer as a result. You should be adaptable and constantly seeking change. You must avoid the urge to overreact or feel sorry for yourself if the change is pushed upon you. Of course, you will want to discover a new method to use your acquired knowledge and expertise rather than discard them. You are focused on the present, not the past. Such imaginative changes frequently jolt people out of comfort and encourage them to reevaluate their course, leading to a better path. Remember that your life's task is living the way your inner self is directing you.

You need to approach your career and its inescapable changes in the following manner: Your devotion is not to a job or an organization, and it is not to a specific position. You are dedicated to completing your purpose in life and giving it your all. You must locate it and give it the proper direction. Others are not obligated to defend or assist you. You are all by yourself. Change is unavoidable, especially in this historically transformative era. Since you work for yourself, it is up to you to anticipate the changes your industry is currently undergoing. Your life's task must be adjusted considering these conditions.

FIND YOUR WAY BACK—LIFE-OR-DEATH STRATEGY

You no longer have to wait for temporal testimony of your thoughts. You believe the reality. You are not allowed to get rid of yourself. You do not belong to you only. You are a part of the universe. You will always be unsure of your significance. But if you put effort into using your experiences to the greatest benefit of others, you can assume that you are doing your job. Deviating from the route you were meant to take will never result in anything good.

Many different types of concealed sorrows will attack you. Most of the time, your deviations are caused by the allure of money and more immediate prospects for success. Your desire will wane, and eventually, the money won't come as easily, because this does not align with anything deep inside you. You will veer off your path as you look for additional, simple ways to make money. You will find yourself stuck in the middle of nowhere if you cannot see clearly ahead of time.

Even if your necessities are covered, you will experience an inner void you need to fill with your beliefs, drugs, or other diversionary activities. At that stage, compromising or escaping the current circumstance is not an option. The intensity of your suffering and annoyance will show you how far you have strayed. You must pay attention to the message of this annoyance and this suffering, and allow it to direct you effectively.

A sacrifice is needed to get yourself back. Leaving the previous course of your life sometimes becomes a source of humiliation and embarrassment. There is no way to have everything now. The path to mastery requires patience; you must focus on the future, five or ten years from now, when you will see the fruits of your hard work. However, this journey has challenges, hardships, and rewards. Make getting back on the right path a goal that you establish for yourself. In the end, those who concentrate on mastery and completing their life's tasks are the ones who will find the wealth and success that genuinely lasts.

TURNAROUND

When faced with limitations rather than strengths and inclinations, the strategy you must take is to overlook your shortcomings and fight the impulse to mimic others. Focus on the little things you accomplish instead. Concentrate on developing these fundamental and useful skills, rather than daydreaming or setting unrealistic objectives for the future. This will boost your self-assurance and serve as a foundation for future ventures. By gradually moving forward in this manner, you will discover your life's ambition.

Recognize that your life's work will not necessarily reveal itself to you in the form of a magnificent or promising desire. It might take the form of your shortcomings, forcing you to concentrate on the one or two things you are unavoidably good at. Working on these abilities will teach you the value of discipline and the benefits of your efforts. Your abilities will spread outward from a center of power and confidence, like a lotus blossom.

Do not be jealous of individuals who seem to have a perfect life. This is frequently a curse, because these people rarely understand the importance of hard work and concentration, and they suffer later in life as a result. Whenever you face obstacles and challenges in your life, take them as an opportunity to make yourself even better and stronger. In these situations, it is typically a good idea to focus on the few things you know and perform exceptionally well, and then regain your confidence.

Something appears to call people toward a specific route sooner or later. You may recall this "something" from your youth as a signal calling when an uncontrollable need, a fascination, or an odd set of circumstances struck like an announcement: "This is what I must do. This is what I must have. I am what I am." This call might have seemed like a gentle push, if not for how vivid and certain it was. Looking back, you might think that fate was involved. A calling may be delayed, evaded, or sporadically forgotten, but it can never be completely diminished.

Regardless of how it calls, it will happen. It will claim its position. Evidently, extraordinary people exhibit calling abilities. Perhaps they are extraordinary because they are devoted to and aware of their mission. Extraordinary people are better witnesses because they can demonstrate what regular people cannot. They appear to be less motivated and more easily distracted. Yet the same universal force propels them toward their destiny.

CHAPTER 3
SETTING THE RIGHT MINDSET

> Study hard what interests you the most in the most undisciplined, irreverent, and original manner possible.

RICHARD FEYNMAN

What distinguishes those who achieve great things in life from those who fail to pursue their dreams? You might guess hard work, inventiveness, a risk-taking attitude, or intelligence. No doubt, these factors also have a critical role in great accomplishments, but the best predictor of success in life is none other than your mindset.

THE IMPACT OF BELIEF SYSTEMS

Beliefs are the long-held attitudes and presumptions people form about themselves, the world, what is possible, what they are capable of, and what they deserve. A person's mindset is the aptitude that impacts how they react to different situations and perceive things. Since beliefs underlie all behavior, a person must first address their assumptions about what is possible before they can talk about learning. People usually pick up this limited thinking from society. People's perception of their potential is initially formed by an experience that gives them a sense of what they are capable of, and it remains fixed after that.

Most people accept the notion about themselves that their potential is limited. In reality, these notions are nothing more than belief systems that you give energy to and allow a place in your mind. You will learn where these lies originate and what you can do to combat them. Although your upbringing and environment may have shaped who you are, you are ultimately responsible for who you become. It's important to realize that your attitudes and presumptions are under your control. And when you acknowledge that you have complete control over your potential, that potential's strength will increase noticeably.

A person meant to achieve great things never loses energy or motivation due to failures or difficult circumstances. People that find success are honest with themselves from the start. No matter the case, they have a positive attitude, engage in constructive growth, and constantly look for ways to improve. Hardships are a part of everyone's lives. Everyone occasionally hears insulting remarks from family members, but the important thing is to be resilient enough to ignore them and move on. Stop listening to someone who continuously criticizes you without reason; they are likely jealous of your development. Keep your focus on yourself and leave the rest behind.

Here I want to pen down my own experiences in life. In my early years, I was frequently labeled as a careless child who was ignorant regarding studies. I was compared to my cousins of the same age in terms of academic performance. I heard terms like "careless," "loser," "stupid," "ignorant," and so on, and I somewhat agreed with those. As time went on, these comments made me furious. At that time, I knew nothing about mindset; all I knew was that I wanted to eliminate these comments. I was not a fan of studies then, but I became tired of hearing such derogatory remarks and decided to prove them all wrong. I put in a lot of effort, and as a result, I eventually outperformed my cousins in terms of academic performance.

I now believe that a bad circumstance occasionally encourages people to step outside of their comfort zone and to try to perform effectively. If those comments hadn't been said to me when I was younger, I wouldn't have worked as hard in school. That became my driving force. However, I want to mention here that this approach is only possible if you have a positive mindset; with a negative mindset, I would have accepted that I am a loser. As I became more aware of the power of learning, my restricting beliefs from earlier in life began to fade. It turned out to be a critical point in my life. I changed from having a constrained mindset and thinking that "things are the way they are" to understanding that I could modify and mold my thoughts to accomplish my objectives. I started thinking about what might be possible and believing in myself for the first time. If you have convinced yourself that you are incapable of reaching your goals, then the secret to becoming limitless is to unlearn the incorrect presumptions that often fail you in reaching them.

THE ROLE PLAYED BY LIMITING BELIEFS IN YOUR LIFE

Limiting beliefs frequently emerge in self-talk, the internal conversation that focuses on persuading yourself what you cannot do rather than what you already do well. It also affects your approach toward your future achievements, because it constantly tries to limit you. How often do you let that voice in your head tell you that something is too difficult for you to attempt, or that you should give up on your goals? If this is how you act and behave, then you are not alone, but you are deteriorating by telling yourself this. People are born into this world with no idea how simple or difficult life will be, how much money will be available, or how valuable they will be. They look at their parents, two experts in every field. Parents are people's first teachers, and they probably didn't plan to hurt their kids. Nevertheless, people carry the limiting views their parents unintentionally placed on them in their early years.

Limiting beliefs can halt your progress, even when performing something you ordinarily excelled at. Have you ever been under pressure to complete a task that usually comes naturally to you, but the strain makes you doubt yourself so much that you lose at this task? That is a restrictive thought that is holding you back. Your inner voice confuses you, but you'd have no issue getting the task done if you could ignore it. Imagine this situation being applied to an entire period of your life. If your limiting beliefs are in control, you will be stuck in underperformance, questioning why you never seem to advance and believing that you don't deserve anything.

These limiting beliefs are like icebergs. You only see a small portion of it, but beneath the sea lies a very deep and strong portion. These beliefs often look small enough to manage, but deep in your consciousness, they are doing great damage that isn't visible from the outside. Iceberg beliefs are strong and ingrained; they feed your emotions. The more deeply embedded this iceberg is, the more damage it causes to your life and inhibits you from taking opportunities. When you achieve control of your icebergs, you will get immense influence over your feelings and your life. When an iceberg melts, all the subsequent events it triggers are also washed away. Here are some tips for reducing limiting thoughts and cultivating a positive attitude.

IDENTIFY YOUR LIMITING BELIEFS

Limiting beliefs frequently emerge in early life. That does not necessarily indicate that your family is responsible for this. Early social environments and educational experiences can both contribute to limiting ideas. Some may take hold simply because something did not go well the first couple of times you tried it as a child. Be aware of how your self-talk is holding you back. Taking the time to investigate the sources of these ideas can be immensely liberating, because once you become aware, you can realize that these thoughts aren't facts about you, but simply opinions. Most of the time, these viewpoints are incorrect. As soon as you recognize them, start talking back to those thoughts that are lingering as your limitations. Tell yourself that even if you were not good at something before, it doesn't mean that you cannot excel in that now. If you ever feel something like this, avoid sharing it with others, because if someone agrees with your doubts about yourself, your self-confidence will drop again.

LOOK FOR THE FACTS

Limiting beliefs prey strongly on emotions. This is one of their most harmful aspects. But finding out whether they are based on facts or just your thoughts can help you eliminate them, which is important for cognitive growth.

Most of the time, people are misguided by their false beliefs. These beliefs misguide people about their potential and capability, but usually, people are not as bad at something as they assume.

Consider a certain situation for yourself. Let's say you will appear for a job interview. Your limiting belief will tell you, "Oh, you are not capable of this; the people competing with you for this job are far better than you. Their CV is stronger, and you will be rejected immediately." If such thoughts are dwelling in your mind, you will start to think about not appearing at that interview because you now believe that you cannot compete. But think about the other side. Aren't all candidates for this job ordinary humans? Why are they more confident than you? If there are ten candidates for a single post, and only one of them will be selected, then why are all others motivated to appear for the interview? Because of their confidence. They don't doubt their caliber, which makes them perform well in front of the interview panel. Even if you fail to convince the panel, take this as an opportunity to learn. Appear in as many job interviews as you can to fight your fear. One day, you will have the self-assurance to stand before them without hesitation. Don't fall apart because of your limiting beliefs.

Think about it like this. You enter the room for an interview, and you are confident. But one question confuses you, and then you start doubting yourself while sitting there. You could become completely distracted from the purpose you went there for. Instead, stay calm and confident, even if you are confused.

For many people, this is an actual problem. The inner critic becomes so distracting while performing something that they lack confidence in, so they are unable to concentrate on it and then perform it poorly. This is one of the reasons it's crucial to discover how to confront and silence your limiting ideas. As you get more adept at this, your ability to limit distractions throughout your toughest growth obstacles will increase. Therefore, when looking at the facts supporting your limiting views, consider whether there is any evidence to support the claim that you are limited in this regard. Or has the chatter in your head polluted the evidence?

ESTABLISH A NEW BELIEF

It's time to make the most crucial move toward developing a new concept, opposite of the lies you have been accepting. This will be helpful to the unfazed version of self you are constructing. You have named your limiting beliefs and carefully examined whether they are true, or just a fabrication of your mind. Now it's time to leave your old beliefs behind. It's time to develop a new belief.

Your inner critic will always lead you if you believe it to be the voice of the truest, most knowledgeable version of yourself. Many people even say things like this: I know myself and what I can and can't do. They have it deeply written in their minds that they are incapable of doing something, which holds them back from even trying. It is because they are not aware of the powers of the magical organ in their head. If you are constantly telling yourself that you can never learn a new language, then you will not give it a try, and thus it will be impossible to learn. But what if you are engaged to someone from another origin, and want to fit into their family and impress them? If you try to learn their language, you will find out that your mind is capable of learning a new language at any time; you just weren't trying before.

What forced you to do something you used to believe you couldn't do? It was the motivation. Motivation shows that you can do anything. So you first need to alter your thoughts and create new beliefs about yourself to quiet down your inner critic. Don't consider it as part of the real you. The better you grow at identifying this voice from the real self, the better you will be at avoiding restricting beliefs.

THE ENDLESS OPPORTUNITIES

Now that you understand how to overcome your limiting beliefs, you can begin to apply your optimistic approach to your journey to achieve limitlessness. Although it may seem like an idealistic strategy, there is a huge amount of research to back up the link between mindset and success. The new perspective you gain from taming your inner critic will open up countless opportunities for you. Positive emotions cause you to see and seize chances that you may not have previously spotted. And you will be well on your way to being infinite if you have a strong sense of motivation and use the appropriate techniques. You will notice how you have confidence in yourself, are more positive toward learning, and have improved your capabilities.

The confidence you gain helps you to conquer anything that comes your way. Try to behave and respond in every situation with calmness. Don't panic and underestimate yourself. There are endless opportunities in front of you once you step out of your comfort zone and allow your thoughts to align with your goals.

I have observed that many people claim that there are no job opportunities and no options for career growth and they feel they are stuck. However, most of the time, they don't even attempt to escape from their shell or make progress. They find it's easy to sit in their chair and complain about the consequences. Therefore, setting a belief about yourself and entering the world to grab opportunities is important. You will find that there are so many options for you in this world, and so many areas to explore once you decide to make the best of your life.

SIX LIES ABOUT LEARNING

Lies are constantly told to you, often by yourself. We are all susceptible to a never-ending flow of inaccurate information about our limitations and skills. Since we hear it so frequently, most of us are forced to accept it as the truth. The issue is that these messages directly contradict the desire to become unlimited. These constrained thoughts we entertain in our minds have the potential to stop us or unpleasantly lead us. I have listed some of the major lies that limit our abilities and that lead our minds to deny any growth in mindset. Let's look at six of these lies.

MISTAKES ARE FAILURE

I have already mentioned in this book that setbacks are part of the struggle, and making a mistake is very normal. Mistakes don't lead to failure; even if you fail your task, you can still get up and start again. The world is not over if you fail.

Let me tell you something: If a person never made a mistake, there is ample chance that they never tried anything unique. Do you know why people worry about making blunders so much? They were evaluated based on their mistakes as students, and their number of mistakes on any given test decided whether they passed the test. Most people were too ashamed to raise their hands again in class once they were humiliated for answering wrong. Unfortunately, mistakes are frequently used to gauge a person's talents, rather than as a tool for learning. Instead of encouraging children to improve themselves in the areas where they are making mistakes, they're scolded and humiliated, which stops them from trying for fear of doing something wrong.

We must change this concept about making mistakes. The fear of making mistakes prevents far too many of us from performing to our full potential. Take your mistakes as evidence that you are trying, rather than viewing them as evidence of failure. A very successful friend of mine explained to me how she and her team were able to view their mistakes not as failures, but rather as significant learning opportunities that resulted in the creation of a new line that advanced their business. They questioned themselves about what they had learned rather than concentrating on their failures.

Always remember that errors don't imply failure. Making errors is a sign that you are trying. You might feel like you need to be faultless, but in reality, life is more about evaluating who you are today as opposed to who you were yesterday. Your ability to grow from your mistakes and become a better version of yourself depends on how well you can learn from them. Furthermore, remember that your faults do not define you; they don't define your personality. Rather, how you cope with them defines you. It's easy to assume that you have no intrinsic value, but "to err is human." Use your mistakes like steps on the ladder to advance to the next level by placing them beneath your feet.

ONLY A CERTAIN PERCENTAGE OF THE BRAIN IS USED

Almost everybody has heard this lie. Many people believe that only a certain percentage of the brain is used, and the rest of the brain remains unused throughout life. Many movies are also based on this idea, but the reality is quite different. This is just a myth to fascinate people into imagining what a human brain could do if it had the power to use 100 percent of it. A person uses their entire brain, and various brain regions govern various functions. If a certain part of the brain is damaged, then other parts take the role of controlling the function that was previously controlled by the damaged part. So the whole brain is involved in the smooth functioning of the body.

I want you to know that you can use your whole brain's capacity. You already have access to the ideal situation that these films and television programs portray. While everyone utilizes their cognitive power, some people use it more efficiently than others. Just as every one of us uses the entire body to perform daily tasks, some of us are more energetic, stronger, tougher, and more fast-paced.

Once you overcome these lies, you will have the knowledge and skills necessary to use your brain as efficiently and effectively as possible.

NEW THINGS CANNOT BE LEARNED

How often have you been impressed by someone doing gymnastics or other sports? But you immediately tell yourself that this is not your cup of tea. Here is a secret: You have infinite potential, and you can learn any sport at any time, provided that you're capable with your health.

When talking about learning, school usually comes to mind. Even when people excelled in the classroom, school was often a place where they faced severe boredom and the growing pains of youth. For those who suffered in school, the feeling of guilt, uncertainty, and the persistent belief that they cannot learn anything was also present. It makes sense that pain and struggle come to mind when people think about learning. Thus, they deceive themselves into believing that learning new things is exceedingly difficult.

Although learning won't always be simple, the effort is

worth it. Learning needs to be difficult; otherwise, you just repeat what you already know. If you have ever attempted to cut wood with a dull blade, you know how much longer and more effort is required to complete the work than when using a sharp blade. Similarly, insufficient approaches or a lack of drive would cause you to think that learning is more difficult than it is. The secret is to move slowly. Consider a big block of wood, and you are trying to cut it. You are fully aware that you cannot chop it all at once. What will you do? You will use a blade and start cutting it; eventually, you will split it in half.

It is not possible to learn everything at once. It takes time; it's a whole process. You need to be slow and consistent. You will need to develop patience, maintain a good mindset, and be adaptable to your demands. It is wonderful if you are a student who benefits from holding a book in your hands. But if this technique does not work for you, why do you keep trying the same thing? Find alternative learning techniques that are effective for you. It won't be as challenging as you think, but it will require some effort.

You will be a better person because you are trying based on the knowledge that you have gained. The truth is that learning new things might be challenging at times. You must also realize that learning is a process that can unquestionably be made easier if you know how to do it accurately.

INTELLIGENCE IS FIXED

Students with a fixed mindset think that their fundamental skills, like intelligence and capabilities, are fixed traits. Once they reach a particular point, they are satisfied with it and always aim to appear intelligent and never foolish. Students with a growth mindset know that their skills can be improved with work, quality instruction, and perseverance.

While they may not think everyone can excel in academics, they think everyone can improve their performance with effort.

Intelligence is never fixed. You can improve it over time, with simple brain exercises and games. If someone truly feels that improvement is impossible, it will not be possible. When you initially think something is impossible, it is quite tough to make progress.

Most people don't consider whether they have a fixed or a growth attitude. Many people continue to think in the same ways as their families, unaware of it. They don't dare to change their thinking patterns. They believe that what they have been told is true. Whether it's the family religion or their political thoughts, they never question them. People will love the person their parents told them to love, and they will hate the person their family tells them to hate. They never question these things, and it makes their thinking limited. The fixed perspective holds that nothing can be changed, because it's just how things are.

Anything can be enhanced if you adopt a growth attitude. Start by assessing your attitude and asking questions. Pay attention to how you speak; a stuck perspective frequently manifests in how you speak. You might think, "I'm not proficient at this thing." This assertion implies that you think your abilities are fixed and cannot be improved. Say something encouraging instead. Try saying, "Maybe I can excel in this in the future." You can use this linguistic change to get better at anything. Your future is not dependent on test results. What you are capable of learning and doing is not determined by them. So don't just focus on gaining marks in exams to prove yourself a genius; instead, try to learn everything. Remember, genius can only be developed via actual practice. It is not a talent you are given at birth.

OTHER PEOPLE'S OPINIONS MATTER

The greatest tragedy in the world is people denying and limiting themselves from expressing who they truly are because they are terrified of what other people will say. Children are the world's fastest learners because they don't care what other people think of them. They don't feel bad about making mistakes. When learning to walk, they will trip and fall countless times, but they won't feel ashamed because they only know they want to walk and don't care about the world around them. It gets harder for people to keep this adaptability as they get older. They may enroll in a singing lesson or a coding course, and if they make a mistake while learning, they might withdraw or stop. Learning to let go of the worry that other people will judge you is a necessary part of becoming infinite. Throughout history, there are examples of people who overcame unfavorable perceptions of those around them. Every successful person has faced criticism in their life. They were bullied, mocked, and degraded, which sometimes depressed them. But they stayed consistent with their goals.

Many people are afraid to try new things because they are worried about what other people will say. Sometimes, people's comments are so degrading and disappointing simply because they don't believe something is possible. Making the life you want can be frightening. Do you know what's worse, though? Regret. One day, you will take your last breath, and neither your anxieties nor the views of others will matter. The only thing that will matter at that time is your satisfaction, and if you lived your life according to your desires. No matter what you do, people will criticize you. You will never realize your true potential if you continue to evaluate yourself unfairly. Don't let other people's thoughts and expectations govern your life or wreck it.

KNOWLEDGE IS POWER

"Knowledge is power" is a saying that's frequently used to justify learning and imply that knowledge alone will provide people with power. Alternatively, you may have heard this expression used to justify keeping facts or knowledge about another person from them, like during a negotiation.

The fact is that knowledge is nothing without action. If you don't dare to take any actions and you don't have a tendency to follow your dreams based on that knowledge, then you don't have any power. Although knowledge is essential, its effectiveness depends on the performance of action. This is where we, as a culture, get bogged down. As mentioned previously, people are constantly overwhelmed with information. Despite having greater access to knowledge than at any other time in human history, taking action becomes more challenging due to the abundance of information.

I once considered this myth to be true. When I was a child, all I wanted was to be able to learn just like the other children in my class. But once I could accomplish that, I soon understood that information alone wouldn't set me apart from those around me; rather, it was how I used knowledge. It is useless if you keep reading this book but do not apply anything to your daily life. Knowledge is only capable of being powerful if you use it properly.

CHAPTER 4
BUILDING THE RIGHT MOTIVATION

 Every act of conscious learning requires the willingness to suffer an injury to one's self-esteem. That is why young children, before they are aware of their own self-importance, learn so easily.

THOMAS SZASZ

Motivation is a set of pleasant and unpleasant feelings that serves as the driving force behind human behavior. Its source is a purpose, a deep sense of the effects of a person's activities, and associations with those effects are the sources of motivation. Contrary to popular opinion, motivation is not fixed, much like your thinking. Everyone's level of motivation is different. When people say that they aren't motivated to do anything at all, they may be motivated to stay in bed all day, snacking and watching TV.

When people tell themselves that they lack motivation, they cast a spell that will not allow them to do anything, because they have programmed their minds this way. Telling yourself, "Today, I have the motivation to do something," won't help much. This is because motivation is not something that comes to you for just a second. It is not something you get for a few hours when you watch a TED talk, and then you become dull again. Rather, motivation is a behavior. It's the behavior that organizes your daily routine and tasks. These small daily tasks contribute toward a bigger goal.

A consistent motivation that determines your life pattern and goals is something that combines purpose, energy, and simple, basic steps. You feel more energized when you have a purpose or reason. You can cultivate energy for your brain and the rest of your body through your practices, and taking action only requires a little energy. Motivation to act is driven by purpose, which must be obvious enough for you to understand. It's crucial to generate enough energy, because you won't be able to act properly if you're sleepy, exhausted, or have a cloudy head.

HAVE THE APPROPRIATE GOAL

Defining the right goal for your life is crucial. If you work hard but do not have a defined direction or motivation for the goal, you will get tired of your struggle and end up empty handed.

When I was younger, I worked extremely hard to compensate for my lack of talent to show everyone I was also capable. But why did I keep working so hard once my learning had advanced, despite being worn out and sleep-deprived? In my most challenging circumstances, I've questioned why I carry on doing what I do. Why exert effort when I can just as easily tell myself that I lack the necessary energy? The truth is that people's greatest challenges frequently result in their greatest abilities.

Also, I have to get extremely clear about my goals, who I am, what I stand for, and why I do what I do every day. These goals align my life in a pattern and keep me motivated all the time. You set priorities and are quite clear about your commitments and their reasons. Identifying the right goal is not that difficult if you follow some simple steps. To help you identify your life goals and the right motivation, I have broken down the steps for you to follow.

ASK YOURSELF "WHY?"

Realizing your life's purpose enables you to live in a better way. People aware of their life's mission are aware of who they are. Furthermore, living a life loyal to your basic principles is simpler when you are aware of who you are. Your major life goals and the explanations for getting out of bed each morning make up your life purpose. A feeling of purpose can control behavior, shape goals, provide a sense of direction, and give life meaning.

People frequently mix the meaning of passion and purpose. However, in my experience, purpose and passion are not the same thing; rather, one fuels the other. Passion returns when people rediscover their true selves—not for those who have been silenced and buried under a mountain of other people's expectations.

To summarize, passion is what ignites your inner flame. You're here to let the world know what you're here for. It matters how you apply your passions. When it comes down to it, everyone exists for the same reason—to use their passions to benefit others. When people get something out of their passion, they will want to share it with the world, and will feel that it is the most important responsibility they have in life.

Reasons pay off when it comes to undertaking anything in life. Even in the face of the daily difficulties that life places in your path, your motivation to act will be sufficiently sparked by factors related to your purpose, identity, and values. All of the work you complete has a purpose, even the unpleasant work. There is a high risk that you haven't identified the purpose behind your activities if you're having trouble finding the motivation to learn or complete other tasks in your life. How can your enthusiasm, desired personality, and ideals serve as the foundation for your claims? You already know that you are far more likely to remember things when you are determined to do so.

It is not a surprise that you want to accomplish your goals, whether that's learning a new sport, learning a new language, staying in shape, or organizing your room. But how do you accomplish this? Establishing smart goals is one of the common methods. The difficulty for many people is that, despite being logical, this procedure is highly complex. Ensure that your objectives align with your emotions to put them into action. Your goals should be as listed.

Specific: Your goal must be specific and defined. Don't say something that gives you a vague idea about your goals.

Measurable: To measure the goal is to define a reference for it. You can assess your advancement using that reference.

Actionable: Devise a proper plan toward your goal. List all of the necessary measures, both big and small, that you must take to achieve your goal.

Realistic: Don't wish for something unrealistic if you cannot do something toward that. Understand that just imagining a situation will not help you achieve your aim.

Time-based: While devising the plan and defining all the steps toward your goal, assign every step its own respective time. Following the timeline is very important when organizing and defining your goal.

Healthy: Your goal must be good for your mental and physical health. Analyze how your goal is contributing to your health.

Enduring: The purpose in life is such a powerful thing that it should make you resilient enough to fight against any unwanted circumstances so that you never leave it in the middle.

Alluring: Your goal must be something for which you should feel excited. If you are not excited about something, how will you motivate yourself to get out of bed and work toward it?

Relevant: A goal must be related to the real-life challenges you have had in your life. It will motivate you more because you will be passionate about fighting against your insecurities.

The legend of King Arthur pulling the sword from the stone symbolizes discovering oneself. The sword represents one's true identity, while the stone represents the obstacles that prevent us from discovering it. In order to remove the sword, Arthur had to have faith in himself and his abilities, just as one must have faith in their own abilities and be willing to take risks to discover oneself. The story teaches us that this journey requires courage, determination, and faith in oneself, and can ultimately lead to a greater sense of purpose and fulfillment.

DEFINE YOUR "I AM"

How you think about yourself will greatly impact your life. Consider two words: I am. Now put anything after these two words that you can connect to yourself; this will define your fate. Note all the specifications of goals that were previously mentioned while defining yourself, because this will greatly impact your life.

You will feel tremendous power when you deliberately choose to identify the habit or objective you want to attain, or consciously leave anything you no longer desire. It's time to start telling yourself, "I am a speedy and effective learner," if you have been telling yourself your entire life that you are a slow learner or incapable of anything. The strongest force in the universe and the ultimate motivation is to act according to your self-perception and put it to good use.

FIND VALUES THAT ARE IMPORTANT

Next, think about your values. Even if you create the most well-planned habits, you won't stick with them if your values conflict. There must be some connection between your actions and values for a motivation to exist.

Values typically don't change unless there is a big, unusual event in your life. Conflict can emerge when you are uninformed of your values and the values of those closest to you. Suppose that freedom and exploration are among your priorities. But if someone in your family values security more than adventure, then there is a high chance that you will frequently disagree with them. Both of these views are correct in their perspectives; the problem is that they are not in harmony. Or suppose you both place high importance on respect, but your definitions of what constitutes respect or contempt vary. Unless you've discussed what respect is, there's still potential for dispute.

For example, if you want to become a singer or an actor and are raised in a society where these professions are not respected, you might lose motivation. There are some conservative societies where people don't encourage these arts. You have a good voice and love to sing for your friends, but your family will still not allow you to adopt it as your profession. The only way is to go against your family's choices, but there is a high chance that you might lose motivation along the way because of constant pressure and rejection of your choice.

WHAT WILL YOU LOSE?

Many people experience fatigue and exhaustion today. I believe this is because everyone thinks they have to accept every invitation or request that comes their way. While it's wonderful to have an open mind and look for various options, you need to be wary when you say yes. Are you sacrificing other needs of yours? Look for what you have to lose when taking on an opportunity.

Losing anything is associated with pain. Pain can teach you many things if you use it as your teacher rather than letting it control your emotions. Utilize suffering as motivation to take action. Make a list of all the advantages and rewards you will experience after any suffering you bear in the process of learning. Identify the things that will genuinely inspire and motivate you, and make a list of them. Once more, be certain that your arguments are strong enough to elicit true feelings. You must genuinely persuade yourself with the advantages of learning any particular skill you are interested in.

ATTRACT THE APPROPRIATE ENERGY

It takes trying new things and immersing yourself in new situations to discover your passion. But if you nurture limited thoughts, they will hinder your progress, and they can also kill your passion. If you have had any unpleasant experiences in your life before, it is the right time to look for what inspires you to identify your passion and immediately switch your focus there. You will certainly find something that will lighten up your mood and will give you the true purpose of your life.

The energy is what drives you, your brain, and your motivation. Therefore, attracting the right energy means you are directing yourself in the right direction, the way you feel a longing for. Building the right energy for your tasks may not be easy, but you can achieve great results with slight effort and consistency. The brain is the main driving force behind a person's actions and motivations; therefore, investing in your brain ultimately attracts positive energies toward you.

Here are my top suggestions for obtaining endless mental energy.

HAVE CLEAN SURROUNDINGS

You might not be aware of how your environment affects your mental well-being. Your brain's work depends on the air you breathe and your surroundings. Some people are so untidy that they believe it is just how they live and don't want to change it. Their room and belongings are dirty, and they refuse to acknowledge that this affects their brain health. However, in reality, as you would feel suffocated in a smoke-filled room, a disordered environment will suffocate your thinking. Cleaning your room will help you feel more relaxed and ease your mind. You'll feel lighter and be better able to concentrate if you clear out the clutter and distractions from your room.

GET BRAIN NUTRIENTS

Brain performance can be optimized by providing the brain with premium food. Consuming nutritious foods rich in vitamins, minerals, and antioxidants nourishes the brain and guards it against the "waste" created when the body utilizes oxygen. When forced to operate on substandard fuel, your brain cannot perform to its full potential. For instance, refined sugar causes inflammation, impairs brain function, and even has the potential to cause depression. The optimum functioning of the human brain necessitates forty-five different nutrients. While the brain produces most of these nutrients, the others come from diet.

Nutrients are best obtained from organic foods. Consult a trained health professional to find out what you could be lacking, and try to make up for it with organic foods. However, you might purchase supplements if you cannot get natural sources of all of these nutrients. The phospholipid DHA, B vitamins, and curcumin are some of the most significant nutrients for the brain.

SURROUND YOURSELF WITH POSITIVE PEOPLE

As discussed earlier, the people around you greatly affect your thinking and motivation. Similarly, this influences your brain health. Your brain's potential is connected to your social networks, like your biological and neurological networks. Spending time with others shapes who you become. Nobody can disagree that the people in your life will greatly impact you.

Your brain's functioning is significantly influenced by the individuals you spend time with.

They certainly impact your inner dialogue, as most people link at least some of their beliefs to those of others. But other people can impact anything, including your eating habits, exercise routine, and even how much sleep you get. Just take a moment to think about who your peers are, how much of an impact they have on your life, and how this affects your desire to be unlimited, so you can better understand where you are now.

MANAGE STRESS

To lessen the physical toll that stress has on your body, the hormone cortisol is released whenever you are under stress. If this occurs infrequently, it's not a concern, but if it occurs frequently, the cortisol buildup in your brain may cause it to stop working correctly. Your thinking will become foggy, and you will not be able to focus on anything. Managing stress and keeping yourself calm in a situation you cannot control brings your personality toward equilibrium.

When the brain is constantly under stress, it seems to build up in the area of the brain responsible for handling threats while devoting less attention to areas of the brain responsible for creativity. Finding techniques to lessen or avoid stress is essential, given the overwhelming evidence that stress can be detrimental to your brain. Learning stress management is necessary for the brain to function properly.

EXERCISE

Exercise is crucial if you wish to free your mind from mental restraints. The brain is altered by exercise in ways that preserve memory and thinking abilities. Have you ever felt sharper while moving? Many students learn their lessons while walking. Similarly, you may have seen people walking forward and backward when they are planning for something. This is because physical activity and mental function are directly related. The hippocampus, a part of the brain involved in language, memory, and learning, appears to grow larger with regular aerobic activity. Aerobic exercise refers to physical activity that raises the heart rate and the body's oxygen consumption.

Try to start your day with light exercise; it helps make you fresh in the morning and stay awake and productive throughout the day. Making this a regular practice will have a significantly positive impact on both your mental and physical health.

SLEEP

Good sleep contributes a lot to brain health. You must get enough sleep to be more focused and think more clearly. You must sleep enough to make wiser choices and remember things more clearly. The proper amount of restful sleep at the right times is just as crucial to survival as access to food and water. It is more difficult to focus and respond quickly when you are sleep deprived because you cannot build or maintain the neural pathways in your brain that allow you to learn and make new memories. Sleep is crucial for the various brain processes, including how nerve cells connect with one another.

According to recent research, sleep has a cleaning function that clears the brain of toxins accumulated while awake. Obtain adequate sleep to utilize your brain to its full potential. For an adult, around seven to eight hours of sleep is necessary. You can take this sleep in fractions or a continuous pattern. But be sure never to deprive your body of sleep. The link between sleep deprivation and various mental and physical illnesses is becoming clearer with advancements in research, including increased sadness, irritability, impulsivity, cardiovascular disease, and other conditions.

KEEP LEARNING

Learning new things also makes your brain more adaptable and strong. It makes our brain healthy by expanding its capabilities. This implies that people continue to build new neural connections in their brains as they learn new things. People keep their brains flexible and pliable to process new knowledge in useful ways. This is especially true if they provide themselves with genuine challenges during learning. Learning a new skill, learning a new language, or embracing aspects of their own culture or other cultures unfamiliar to them are things that can stimulate new neural connections in the brain. Your brain's capacities expand as you increase the ways you employ them.

KILL NEGATIVE THOUGHTS

Like most individuals, you set boundaries for yourself by thinking negative things. Perhaps you persuade yourself that you lack the intelligence to master a talent you truly want to have. Or perhaps you keep repeatedly saying that pushing yourself to success only results in disappointment. For the best development of your brain, try to stay as far away from these thoughts as possible. Because if you start to justify your thoughts, you will start believing in them and become a negative person. You won't do something if you constantly tell yourself that you cannot, that you're too old, or that you lack the intelligence to do it. You can only successfully achieve your goals after you stop engaging in this negative self-talk.

FOLLOWING A SIMPLE SET OF STEPS

Now that you have defined your life's purpose, you have a motive or goal. You have the potential to compete for it. A modest, easy step is the smallest thing you can do to advance toward your aim, one that takes little effort or power. These little steps matter. These become habits over time. People often feel overwhelmed by the amount of work that needs to be done, which is one of the main reasons they don't dare to take action. A task or job may appear so huge and time-consuming that you cannot envision how you will ever complete it. When a project is considered as a whole, people will often conclude that the task is too hard, so they stop or postpone it. Procrastination and incomplete tasks frequently result in negative thought patterns. These patterns can interfere with sleep, cause symptoms of anxiety, and negatively affect a person's physical and psychological abilities. Instead of looking at a task as a whole, only take small steps that don't move you away from your goal or make you lose motivation.

BE KIND TO YOURSELF

If your goals appear impossible to fulfill in a short time, don't rush to do them. Give yourself time to work on them and break them into manageable portions. Be kind to yourself whenever you feel down. If you feel terrible about your inability to complete a task on time, then you might start to feel bad about it and lose all your motivation. If you have any uncompleted work, then it might cause mental anxiety. Adding guilt and shame to this makes it considerably more difficult to complete a task and will make you miserable.

You're already feeling bad about it, and this is painful. But once this feeling controls your thoughts, your thinking becomes vague, and focusing on anything will be impossible, making you even more unproductive. It will take time away from you while you feel horrible about your profession, time that you could be spending with friends and family or doing something else enjoyable. It will probably be more difficult to stop procrastinating if you feel guilty about your lack of advancement. Take a break, then devise a pattern to eliminate procrastination, and any guilt associated with it. Give yourself some breathing room, no matter what is up next.

TAKE BABY STEPS

Three things have the power to alter someone's behavior. The first is to experience inner enlightenment. The second is to modify your environment, which is possible for almost everyone. The third is to move slowly.

Making gradual progress is one of the main things that will influence your behavior. You might have heard the story of the rabbit and the tortoise. What does that story tell you? A slow-paced tortoise beat the fast-paced rabbit in a race because it was slow and consistent. People often rush to see the results of their efforts, and they often try to take large steps, which later become hard for them to cope with. Therefore, it is better to take small but consistent steps.

The way to complete a task you are putting off can be made simple by dividing it into manageable bits. Get started on finishing the assignment, because until you do it, you won't be able to put your mind at ease about it. Assign any starting point—the point where it might be easy for you. Get started by making up your mind to finish it. Even if you don't have the energy or motivation to do it all, you will appreciate yourself if you divide this into small steps and start to accomplish them step by step.

PUT YOURSELF ON AUTOPILOT

Putting yourself on autopilot means doing things in a very effortless way. It happens when you do something habitually. Repeated, small, easy steps form habits, defining a person's daily routine. According to numerous studies, around 50 percent of what people do each day is the result of an established habit. This means that it is automatic, that people don't have to think about most things, yet people do them for a major part of their days.

Consider all the routine tasks you complete each day without much thought. Setting your room after waking up, eating breakfast, brushing your teeth, and checking your phone now and then is something you do automatically. You don't have to tell yourself to do it. After returning from the office, you walk into the room, change your clothes and hang them, take out your comfy clothes and put them on, jump into bed, and turn on the TV. During this time, you might be thinking about some meeting in the office, but you are not giving a single thought to what you are doing.

Your daily routines mainly determine your wellness, prosperity, and pleasure. Knowing how to alter your habits encompasses how to confidently control your days and concentrate on the actions that have the greatest influence on your life. A key method of simplifying your life and actions that you do unconsciously and frequently is to develop habits to automate tasks.

Now that you are on the path to becoming unlimited, you know that maintaining bad habits depletes your superpowers. How you break harmful habits and, more importantly, how you establish new and helpful behaviors is very important when influencing your mindset.

GET IN THE HABIT OF LEARNING

It is generally accepted that changing a negative habit involves substituting it with a new and more positive habit rather than just eliminating the old one. Starting a new habit is considerably simpler than stopping an old one without finding a replacement. Suppose you don't replace your old habit that you want to change with a better one. In that case, you will have difficulty getting rid of it because you will have a longing for that habit. That is why replacing it with another habit that's better than the previous one is more helpful.

Of course, no one could survive without habits, but actively attempting to replace destructive habits with positive ones will boost your powers to a new level. How determined you are to stop the particular habit is the main factor. A new habit is simpler to break than an old one; therefore, its time-line should also be considered. Also, why do you want to break that habit, and how will it affect your life if you don't break it?

A person needs to be sufficiently motivated, competent and effectively encouraged for a target behavior. For the behavior to occur, you need the motivation to do it. It is extremely difficult to develop a habit out of something you don't truly want to do. You also need the necessary abilities because it is impossible to develop a habit out of something you cannot do. Take a look at factors that cause motivation.

Pleasure and pain: Pleasure and pain are the greatest motivators for any actions you are going to take. Think of anything you want to achieve; you often imagine the pleasure associated with it, which motivates you. Similarly, the dread of pain also boosts motivation for certain actions in life.

Hope and fear: When you have hope, you expect something good to happen; when you are fearful, you expect the opposite. Although it sounds more or less like a pain/pleasure motivator, it is something more powerful than that. For example, in some situations, people accept pain to overcome fear.

Social acceptance and rejection: Everyone wants to be socially acknowledged, which is part of human behavior. People want to be accepted by their fellows, friends, and family, and they fear being rejected by others. These feelings act as a very strong motivator.

REDEFINE YOUR ABILITY

Human ability is infinite, but they prefer looking for something that they find simpler and can do with more interest. Thus, human ability can often be equated with simplicity. The simpler that something is for a person, the more they feel they can do it. I have listed some of the categories of simplicity.

Time: The more time someone has, the more confident they are in performing a certain task, but if a deadline is approaching, they start to panic and feel that they cannot cope with the task.

Money: When a person wants to do something that demands money, then they won't consider it to be simple, unless they have abundant financial resources.

Physical effort: People are more inclined toward tasks requiring less physical effort.

Brain effort: Just like with physical effort, people look to ease their minds by avoiding mentally tiring tasks.

Social deviance: Because of social norms, it is hard to follow that path because people fear social rejection.

If you want to become limitless, you need to enhance your abilities by liberating yourself from these constraints. Instead of satisfying your mind with simpler and easier tasks, try some tasks that require little effort. Little by little, you will improve yourself, enhance your ability, and feel more confident dealing with tougher tasks. Understand all these categories of simplicity, and challenge yourself in every category to become better at managing time and saving money. Be a little hard on yourself by exhausting yourself with physical and mental effort and liberating yourself from the thoughts of being rejected by the people around you. You will soon find that you are better able to deal with anything.

CREATE NEW HABITS

Most people know that developing good habits is essential

to their development, and that the only way to break bad habits is to replace them with healthier ones. But how exactly can you develop a habit?

- Make sure that you genuinely desire to make something your habit. Making something a habit gets challenging if you are not genuinely interested in it.
- Is the new habit you are trying to develop compatible with your unique abilities? Keep in mind that if something is continually tough for you to accomplish, it is unlikely that you will develop it into a habit.
- Set up a reminder for yourself to start the new behavior right away. Do not rely on tomorrow. Now is the time to act on it.

ADOPT ONE HABIT AT A TIME

We have already discussed the importance of taking small steps to achieve big things. The same rule applies to building habits. You might believe that your repeated failures to alter your routines and behaviors have made you a lifelong loser. But the amount of progress you can make by altering just one or two basic daily routines is extraordinary. You will find that basic daily routines play a big role in building constructive habits. Even something as simple as using the other hand to clean your teeth can begin a new way of living.

DESIGN A DAILY ROUTINE

Why does your morning routine matter so much? I firmly believe that you will have a significant edge if you begin your day by giving your brain a jumpstart with a series of easy activities. Additionally, by creating effective routines early in the day, you may benefit from them throughout the entire day. You might have heard about the term *inertia* in physics. Just like the inertia of the body, there is the inertia of a successful routine; once you have something going, you can keep it going with much less effort than if you were starting from zero. To make your whole day productive, it is better to start your day energetically.

Before I even get out of bed, I plan my whole day and reflect on the day before. I think about and devise strategies on how I can make myself more productive today. I plan one and two hours of my morning while lying in bed. When I get out of my bed, I do all those tasks in the time I have assigned to them. You can also change yourself with little effort.

I first make my bed and fold my blanket in the morning when I get out of bed. This is my day's first success, and successful habit. It's a simple achievement with the extra benefit of making my bedtime more enjoyable because it's always wonderful to come home at night to see my bed is all set. Making the bed first thing in the morning is a habit taught to soldiers because it prepares them for success in all they have to tackle.

After waking up, I drink a large glass of water. Because bodies lose a lot of water while sleeping just from breathing, hydration is crucial first thing in the morning. I then use the opposite hand to clean my teeth. I do this to train my brain to perform challenging tasks, as it engages a different brain region and compels me to be present.

After that, I run in a nearby park and work out there for ten minutes. Even though this isn't my whole workout, I still want to raise my heart rate first thing in the morning because it promotes oxygen flow to all body parts, particularly the brain. It also helps to improve my sleep pattern and weight control. I continue by engaging in breathing exercises to oxygenate my body. I love to do yoga and meditation in the morning. It increases my positive energy and prepares my mind for the day ahead. When I return home, I take a bath, followed by a healthy breakfast, and then I am ready to go to work. These simple activities prepare me for a day full of achievements and success.

My midday routine is straightforward: I work out for a while to make me feel refreshed after hours of office work. Then I take lunch, check emails, and check my bank accounts. After these activities, I take a short nap, which restores my energy for the rest of the day.

Before hitting the bed at night, I check the financial transactions of my company to have a record of them with me whenever I am in need. Then I rearrange things in my room because it helps me to feel good knowing that everything is in its place when I wake up in the morning. I take a night bath, and then go for six to seven hours of sleep. There is no dinner for the evening routine. That's because I'm doing reverse-intermediate fasting, where I don't eat dinner and break my fast with breakfast. I consider it a very healthy routine because, at night, my body is at low energy, and the metabolism rate is also low; therefore, fasting at night is a good idea. The next day, I eat a good breakfast because I need more energy to work all day.

Between my morning, midday, and evening routines is the time for creativity, where I do all my work and spend time acquiring any new skill in which I am interested. See how straightforward and organized my routine is? I have reduced the distractions in my life, and I have planned every minute of my day, which helps me become more productive while taking care of my health.

OTHER SMALL HABITS TO PRACTICE IN A DAY

Reading: Build a habit of reading. It is essential for cognitive development, and it broadens your thinking patterns. Along with learning many new things, reading daily for about an hour can have many other impacts. For example, it will also give you the knowledge and confidence to speak in public because you have authentic knowledge of the subject.

Walking: If you can't or don't want to get yourself into a tiring workout, thirty-minute walks are another healthy habit. Make a routine of walking for thirty minutes only. You can go to a nearby market on foot instead of driving. Make a habit of this; it will positively impact your brain and body.

Kindness to others: We have already talked about being kind to ourselves in this book. What about practicing kindness and love for other people? Becoming more loving and caring toward people is a great habit. See if anyone out there is in need. If you are in a position to help them, don't hesitate to do them a favor.

Writing: Along with reading, writing is also a great habit that involves different parts of your brain. Start writing your daily activities in a journal. Mention all the small and big events that made your day. Mention your achievements and losses in that diary, and try to improve by noting your flaws.

Saving: Nowadays, people are trying to stay so up-to-date with fashion and other trends that it is almost impossible for them to save anything. But saving a small portion of money can be very helpful to you in the future. It will make you confident, as you will not rely on others for sudden financial assistance. Furthermore, if you find that these savings are more than enough for you, you can donate some of them to charity, which will help you to help those in need.

CHAPTER 5
RELYING ON LIMITLESS METHODS

66 He who learns but does not think, is lost! He who thinks but does not learn is in great danger.

CONFUCIUS

earning methods include any activities that are consciously done, or using materials made available to aid learning at the individual, team, or organizational levels. Each student has a technique they adopt when studying to help them retain knowledge more effectively. Some take notes, some draw diagrams, some listen to lectures, and so on. Learning is not just associated with studies; it affects every aspect of people's lives. They continue learning from the cradle to grave, so it is always a good idea to adopt the proper learning methods. In the previous chapters, you figured out how to start each day with a productive mindset and the highest possible degree of motivation. Now let's talk about the learning methodology that separates individuals who are unlimited from those who are constrained by their mental restrictions.

Methods are the steps or processes used to complete a task. In learning, methods refer to means that best help people use the mind to retain the knowledge they have learned. People are taught highly outdated and ineffective learning techniques in the educational system, like rote memorization.

In this section, you will understand the science of rapid learning and meta-learning, which covers five topics in detail. Once you understand these topics and begin using these tools, you'll find how you have been led in the wrong direction your whole life, and you'll be astonished by the possibilities these topics open up for you.

FOCUSING

The secret to unlocking your abilities is to focus more intensely. When you are fully committed to a task and your mind is concentrated, you will do things that seem impossible when your mind is scattered or distracted. Continual distractions make it challenging to stay on task, and these distractions are the main foe of concentration. In today's highly connected world, distractions are only a click away. To learn new things, accomplish goals, and perform well in a variety of settings, you must be able to focus on the task at hand and direct your mental energy toward it.

I'm sure there have been many moments in your life when you have focused entirely on a task. For example, you are all in when you cook your favorite dish, write a letter to a loved one, or paint your imagination on a canvas. This occurs because you can sharpen your attention and focus on the current task.

When you are fully focused, you dive into your task at hand and ignore any outside distractions. But why do many people find it hard to maintain focus? Simply, because this is the result of never having learned how to focus. I don't remember having a class at the primary level where they taught us how to build our focus.

Focus helps people improve their cognitive skills to finish a task swiftly and effectively. You can do remarkable things with a focused mind. In contrast, when you lack focus, you are less likely to succeed because you are not as emotionally or physically devoted to achieving your goals.

PRACTICE CONCENTRATION

Concentration is the capacity to focus on one item for an extended time. It is the ability to direct attention to following your desires. Attention management is a critical component of concentration. It is the capacity to concentrate on a single concept, object, or subject while blocking out all irrelevant thoughts, emotions, and sensations.

The key to all human success is concentration. You cannot manifest if you cannot concentrate. Unfortunately, people aren't taught how to concentrate during their early education. Your parents and teachers might have scolded you for not paying attention if you couldn't concentrate on something. But you were probably never taught how to concentrate.

You can increase your concentration by trying as much as you can. The more you practice, the more you become effective at concentrating on any given task. Every time my concentration wavers, I summon my willpower to regain it. Although it won't be simple at first, making a deliberate effort to use your willpower in this manner is likely to produce remarkable benefits.

CALM DOWN YOUR NERVES

The amount of information you receive daily is likely stressing you out, even if you aren't aware of it. If you're like most people, you might even view this positively, because it indicates that you're engaged and that, through your business, you're having a positive impact on the world. While this might be accurate in a certain way, it also contributes to anxiety. Anxious thoughts can consume you, making it challenging to decide what to do and how to take action to address your troubles. Overthinking can result from stress, which can then result in more anxiety, which can then result in more overthinking, and so on. How do you break free from this troubled cycle?

You can benefit from techniques like meditation, yoga, and certain martial arts to help you relax your busy mind. But if your schedule is very busy and you cannot spare more than a few minutes for the calmness of your mind, then there are a few other simple techniques you can practice. These are the top three:

Breath

Breathing is considered one of the best exercises to relieve stress. Many people work in an overburdened environment for many hours of the day, and sometimes even need to sacrifice sleep for their work. This often makes them feel tired and stressed. If you don't have much time to do proper meditation or yoga, use a deep breath to clear your mind and soul. For this, sit back on the chair and then close your eyes. Take a deep breath, hold it for a moment, and then whoosh it out. You'll feel a lot better if you do this a few times.

Do Your Pending Tasks

Many people put things on a to-do list, but then continue to procrastinate and never do those things. When things start to pile up in your mind, they cause stress. Until you deal with the issues in your mind, they will continue to be a burden. There may be something you need to complete that you've been putting off, which will cause more difficulties with focusing because your mind will be working on a dozen different levels at once. Take care of that challenging task so that you can give more attention to everything else you want to complete.

Allocate Time to Distractions

Turning off your phone, email, or other social accounts might be difficult when you need to concentrate, but it will be excellent if you can persuade yourself to do this.

However, you might get worried because of your duties, and avoiding checking your mail will become complicated. This is why you perceive these things as obligations or problems, making it much more difficult for you to ignore them.

One method to handle this is to address one of your worries directly, but there will be instances in which that will be impossible. Instead, how about assigning a specific time to bring these concerns and commitments to the front of your mind? It's unlikely that merely telling yourself, "I'll worry about that later," will prevent your worry from returning in twenty minutes. However, deciding to worry about it at 9:00 p.m. may be a good idea.

STUDYING

How you approach your education is vital. You must under-stand that limitlessness also involves becoming a student for life. It's necessary to understand this so that you can use these approaches in your learning process. This includes memo-rizing information, highlighting the most significant elements, and perceiving how people learn. You can discover how to broaden your academic horizons. It will be a super-power you use for the rest of your life, once you achieve it.

Most people weren't trained in efficient study techniques. The problem is that most of the methods you currently employ are outdated and inefficient. This is a highly competi-tive information age, where information can be found almost anywhere. But people continue to use the same old tech-niques to digest it all. Learning requirements today are very different from previous times.

The world's most successful people are lifelong learners. That implies that they are constantly picking up new skills, remaining current with developments in their professions, and keeping up with what other fields might have to offer. You should make studying a part of your entire life if you want to achieve your objective of becoming a limitless learner.

WHAT ABOUT CRAMMING?

A lot of people think that cramming is the best method of exam preparation. However, cramming is linked to emotional, behavioral, and physical problems that lessen the body's capacity to be productive. Additionally, cramming often requires students to study all night and sacrifice their sleep.

Skipping a significant portion of your sleep while studying can ruin the purpose of learning in the first place. Nobody says that students shouldn't study, but getting enough sleep is also essential for doing well in school. Working with children of all ages taught me that studying in this way rarely results in better learning.

HABITS THAT ENFORCE LEARNING

You can learn more effectively by adopting these seven easy habits.

Habit 1: Use Active Recall

You should instantly check how much of it you've retained when you review information. This is known as active recall. Most students are unaware of how crucial it is to make themselves recall information. Retrieving information that you are trying to remember is vital for memory development. When studying, make sure you have enough time to perform this procedure repeatedly. An initial learning session that comprises the repeated study and forced-recall assessment of all items produces the best results for learning.

Habit 2: Use Spaced Repetition

Although it is human nature to procrastinate by putting things off, doing so increases the likelihood that you won't retain the content you were trying to learn. The ideal way to use your brain is to space out your memorization of the content. Spaced repetition purposefully manipulates how your brain functions, making it accessible and incredibly amazing at learning. The brain responds to this repetitive stimulus by fortifying the connections between nerve cells, much like muscles do. It results in long-lasting knowledge retention.

Habit 3: Control the Situation You're In

As previously discussed, the state you're in at the time of any activity will have the most significant influence on how successful you are. For instance, you probably won't give your best effort if you have an awful day and then have to make a presentation or take a test. This is because you are not performing at your best due to your mental state. On the other hand, if you have an amazing day, you will undoubtedly do better when the same opportunity is presented to you. The same applies to studies.

Habit 4: Use Your Smell Sense

Another thing that was previously discussed is how a particular scent might bring up memories of earlier times. The sense of smell and its effects on memory can also be employed to improve learning. Put a little essential oil on your wrist while studying for a big test, and ensure you repeat the process right before the test. If you do the same thing when preparing for an important meeting, you should get similar outcomes. This method could be beneficial for memorizing and learning things.

Habit 5: Use Music for the Mind

Consider some of your first learning experiences. Did you memorize the alphabet via a song, like so many other people? Parents have always used music to educate their young children on fundamental concepts. They do it because it works, and it works because it is backed by science. Many researchers have connected music with education. There is a relationship between music and mood and, subsequently, between mood and learning, which suggests that music might enhance people's learning environments. Many rhythms are specially designed for students in order to assist in their learning processes, and you can find them on YouTube and other platforms. Music stabilizes mental, bodily, and emotional states to achieve intense concentration and focus.

Habit 6: Listen Attentively

More than a quarter of people are auditory learners, which means they learn largely by hearing, and there is a strong correlation between listening and learning. Because hearing is so important for learning, people spend much of their waking time listening. But many people aren't very great at it. They frequently fail to focus all of their brain power on the task at hand, which is one of the reasons people have trouble listening with concentration. Try to commit to the situation thoroughly, and look forward to its positive results. If you are in a talk, try to concentrate on what the speaker is telling the audience. If your attention wanders, bring it back. Take notes of the speech and try not to get involved in gossip while listening in order to maintain focus. If you can talk to the speaker in person, take the chance to request further explanation or even a clarification of the idea. Take notes if you have a notebook and a pen with you. And after that, consider what was said. Imagine teaching it to someone else as you say it in your head. This will help to retain it in your brain.

Habit 7: Make Notes for Yourself

The main benefit of taking notes is that they let you enhance your knowledge, memory, vocabulary, and cognitive style. But many people take notes ineffectively. Taking excellent notes will allow you to organize and analyze information that will benefit you when you use them later. One common mistake people make when taking notes is trying to write down everything they hear. Paying too much attention to what they're writing and paying no attention to listening doesn't allow them to make good notes. Make clear objectives before taking notes. Make your notes in a way that makes it easy for you to recall the content later. Use abbreviations and shortcuts that you are comfortable with. Using your own words in your notes helps you process the information, which will significantly improve your learning. After you're done taking notes, quickly go over them. Instead of going back to your notes days later, doing this will significantly improve your ability to recall them. Since the material will still be fresh in your mind, you will be able to rewrite anything you might have forgotten to write down.

MEMORIZING

Everyone needs to memorize things to survive, because we cannot learn or remember anything without memory. Still, people often face hard times while memorizing. The way people were taught to memorize in school was inappropriate. Not only did you probably find it hard to memorize your schoolwork, but you probably also found it torturous. Even today, most schools instruct students to memorize by repeating a fact or a quote until it becomes momentarily ingrained.

Memory benefits you in every area of your life. There are no tasks you can complete without using your memory. Imagine waking up every day and losing all of your previous knowledge. You would have to teach yourself how to rise from the bed, eat, brush your teeth, dress up, and exercise. That would be very annoying.

The majority of brain functions critically depend on memory. You should expand your memory if you wish to give your brain a significant increase in functionality. Let me assure you of this important fact: There is no such thing as a great or poor memory. The fact is that there are two types of memories: trained memories and untrained memories. If you have a hard time remembering things, it isn't because you are unintelligent. Instead, you just lack the necessary training.

Why is memory so crucial if you want to be limitless? Because every action you take now and in the future is built on the foundation of your memory. Consider what it would be like if your computer had limited memory, and how frustrating it would be for you to store data. The majority of tasks would be nearly impossible to complete.

WHY IT IS ESSENTIAL TO IMPROVE MEMORY:

If you are not taking it seriously to work on your memory, you have accepted your current level of memorization. If you are not working on it, there is a lot that you could lose in your life. Let me explain how working on your memory is essential for your lifestyle.

- Memorization disciplines the mind. It improves mental discipline and concentration.
- Sometimes, you don't have access to the Internet. At those times, your memory comes into play.
- Mental capacity is enhanced by memorization. The more you try to memorize, the more open your mind becomes to learning.
- Working memory is where your thoughts are kept, and can only be quickly accessed from the brain's internal memory.
- An active memory helps you to recall almost anything, which makes you smart and intelligent in many encounters.

YOUR CURRENT MINDFULNESS

We've already discussed the significance of memory in practically all brain activities. You must broaden your memory if you want to grow your mind. This requires strengthening your memory so that it can hold a lot of information and provide you with easy access to it. Most people view learning as a passive process. They come across knowledge via books or lectures; if the knowledge is retained, it is excellent! However, if not, they believe there is nothing they can do.

Here I want to mention my friend, who had severe memory issues. She accepted that she was born like this and would live her life like this. She forgot her call letter when she went for an interview. She would leave her car keys inside the car, and she left her passport at home when she went to the airport to catch a flight. These things occasionally happen to most of us, but it was a routine for her. Almost daily, she encountered a disaster and was often referred to as "dumb" and "irresponsible." She told me that no matter how hard she tried to remember, she still forgot one thing or another.

I told her about a few techniques that I practiced and asked her to find which one suited her. She started working on these practices, and soon found she was getting better at memorizing things. She told me that she also searched the web and was working on many ways to improve herself and felt far more confident than before.

I am including these simple ways to enhance memory skills.

Visualization

You have a powerful visual memory. It is easier to remember a tale if you can visualize the images it creates rather than merely reading the words that describe it. The use of images aids in the process of thinking. When there is something that you need to memorize, make a picture of it in your mind so whenever you think about it, that particular picture appears in your mind. It will encourage you to remember more. Remember that a picture really is worth 1,000 words!

Association

Any new information you learn can be retained when it is connected to something you already know. New information must be connected to something you already know by introducing an association between them. Every minute, your mind unconsciously creates numerous associations, and when you consciously do this, it will boost your memory. Do you have a song that reminds you of someone special? It is an association.

Emotion

It is easier to remember something when you add a feeling to it. Information on its own is forgettable, but when mixed with emotion, it is remembered for a longer time. When something is given emotion, it becomes exciting, hilarious, and action-packed, and you are far more likely to remember it.

Location

Memories can also be attached to different locations, and visiting that place later triggers your memory. For example, perhaps you went to a certain monument when you were a kid; if you go there again when you are older, you will see how you remember everything and visualize your mini version.

PRACTICING READING

Reading is one of the best habits that you can grow. There was a time when I hated reading and tried to avoid it as much as possible. But I noticed that all my friends and classmates who had the habit of reading had so much knowledge, along with powerful language skills. I wanted to be like them, but I didn't want to read.

Soon, I realized there was no escape from reading if I wanted to become limitless. So I bought a few novels and digests and started reading them. I found it very hard to comprehend them at first, because I was not used to it, but I challenged myself to be better, no matter what. I kept trying and trying, and soon, I became good at reading and increased my reading speed. Now I have read countless books on various topics.

Reading is good, but speed reading is better. Developing speed reading will help you understand and grasp the book's concepts in much less time than an ordinary person. This does not only apply to book reading. It applies to all other reading processes—for example, taking a test that has a limited time. If you're skilled at speed reading, then you might complete it within the limited time; otherwise, you might not have enough time to complete the reading content. If you want to eliminate these problems, try practicing speed reading.

HOW READING EXPANDS YOUR MIND'S POTENTIAL

Strategies to expand your learning must incorporate reading. Reading is fundamental to almost all learning. But it can be hard to make reading an active and continual part of your life without a determined commitment. Here's why:

- Reading is a demanding and fulfilling exercise for your brain because it requires it to perform several tasks simultaneously. It connects parts of the brain that have developed for other purposes—such as sight, speech, and cognitive processing. Reading provides an unusual amount of mental exercise, and since the brain is like a muscle, it becomes stronger the more you put it to work.

- When you read, your brain performs at a greater level because reading is an excellent mental exercise. Numerous studies have indicated that engaging in activities like reading throughout your life, from childhood to old age, will help keep your brain healthy and your memory sharp for longer.

- When people sit down with a book or even spend some time reading a newspaper, one of the things they are doing is training their minds on this one object. When people read, they often focus almost exclusively on what they're reading, unlike when using something like a social platform.

- Smart people frequently have access to and the aptitude for a more extensive vocabulary than the typical individual. You can naturally increase your vocabulary by reading. As you read more, you are exposed to a broader range of words and their uses in more comprehensive circumstances.

- If you've ever been asked to come up with a story for a task at work or school, you know it is frequently simpler to think creatively when using a tool to get started. A strong imagination opens up more options, and reading stimulates your imagination.

- Reading plays a significant role in developing an understanding of different things. By reading, you can learn about lives you've never had, things you've never imagined, and ways of thinking that are very different from your own. All of this increases your capacity to develop empathy for other people and comprehend how the world functions in general.

HOW TO READ FASTER
Use Your Finger to Guide Your Reading

Using your finger as a guide helps you maintain focus and inhibits your eyes from straying. Because your eye is drawn to motion, reading with your finger accelerates your reading rate. Practice reading by using your fingers. Trace the words with your finger, and don't stress comprehension or keeping track of the time, because this is a practice session. Set the alarm for one minute. Take up where you left off after your initial evaluation. Read until the alarm goes off. Write down your new reading speed after calculating your new reading rate. According to studies, using your finger to read can boost your reading speed by between 25 percent and 100 percent. Your results will improve as you use this strategy more frequently.

Think About Reading Like It's a Work Out

Your "reading muscles" will strengthen if you force yourself to read more quickly, and what was once difficult will become simple. Anyone who exercises regularly can relate to this. If you force yourself to read two or three times faster than usual, your reading speed will significantly improve. Make a proper reading schedule. You cannot expect to build muscle by exercising for just one day, and the same applies to reading. Regular reading is necessary to prevent your reading skills from deteriorating.

Increase Your Field of Vision

The range of characters or words your eyes can see in a single glance is your peripheral vision. You can see and process more words by expanding your peripheral vision. Most people only learned to read one word at a time in school. However, you can read more than that when you are grown up. Skilled readers see clusters of words rather than single words, just as you see words rather than individual letters.

Count

Naturally, reading faster makes it more challenging to speak all the words aloud, or even think about them. It will be hard to subvocalize every word once you have reached a specific reading rate. When you reach this point, your mind will switch from speaking the words to viewing them more as images. It will be more like watching a movie when you read a book. Another method for muting this inner voice is counting. The steps are surprisingly easy: count aloud while you read, saying "one, two, three," and so on. With this technique, you can reduce your subvocalization, increasing your ability to see words rather than hear them. This ultimately enhances your speed and comprehension.

THINKING

It is impossible to excel in something without nurturing your thinking process. New ways of thinking are frequently needed in order to accomplish something significant. People can think to an extent, but they often don't feel the need to improve, and will rely on technologies instead, since these make the effort for them, while they don't need to use their minds. Often, when people are presented with a riddle, after giving it a little thought, they will give up because they can eventually get the answer, and there will be no need to think anymore.

Not only do people need to work on their thinking, but they also need to improve their thinking capacity, exponentially. You may not want to create a billion-dollar corporation, solve all the world's problems, or make a scientific break-through. You will see how using exponential thinking could benefit your everyday life. The next time you face a challenge that requires critical thinking, keep in mind these steps to activate your exponential thinking skills, and take a signifi-cant step toward unleashing your brilliance.

Step 1: Identify and Address the Core Issue

Sometimes, the issue is not what you can see directly; instead, it may be caused by something concealed behind what you can see. The surface issue can be resolved in a far more practical way if the underlying problem is resolved. So if you feel that it's impossible for you to study for an upcoming exam, or it is just too hard for you to grasp the concepts, then there might be some other thing taking your time and making you think this way. Look for the distractions and unnecessary hang ups that are taking up your time and making you think that you are unable to excel. Cut out those distractions, and you will have plenty of time to focus on the subject of your upcoming exam.

Step 2: Look for a New Approach

Thinking in what-if scenarios is one of the secrets to expo-nential thinking. What-if statements introduce unexpected possibilities. For example, what if aliens invade this world? What if Earth suddenly stops revolving around the Sun? What if I was born in some other country or religion? Questions like these trigger the thought process. This helps people envision a variety of things that they might not have otherwise considered, and enables them to think about what might be necessary for them to survive in the future. Consider if your everyday life routine follows the pattern of what your society wants you to do. What would it be like if you followed your passion instead of caring about other people's thoughts? Or perhaps what would happen if the day had 12 hours instead of 24 hours?

Step 3: Read and Read

I always try my best to encourage reading as much as possible. Reading is the activity that frees your thinking from restrictions. When it comes to exponential thinking, reading is crucial. Without a comprehensive understanding of a subject, it is impossible to make significant cognitive leaps. Whatever topic is your subject of study, and whatever what-ifs are associated with it, you should read about it as much as possible. There is plenty of information on every topic, so there are no excuses. There is no way that I will let you escape from reading. So read, read, and read.

Step 4: Extrapolate

You've now determined the root cause of the issue, developed hypothetical scenarios that let you picture life without the issue, and conducted your research. It is high time to extrapolate on this. You will extend your thoughts to the unknown situation that might come in the future, and you will try to assess whether it will be applicable in the future or not. What would happen if you got a job abroad and relocated there with your family? You know that taking such drastic action or progress won't appear immediately. You're aware of all the modifications you need to make, and it might even seem like you've taken a significant step backward. But if you have extrapolated on the situation beforehand, you will get a better idea of how to thrive in an apparently alien environment.

CHAPTER 6
RAPID SKILLS ACQUISITION

> 66 The more that you read, the more things you will know. The more that you learn, the more places you'll go.

DR. SEUSS

To actively compete in today's world, you need to learn the skills that are in high demand. Whether soft or hard skills, you need to know everything related to your field if you want to excel. You can figure out how to speed up the learning process if our mind is open to learning in new and better ways.

The foundation of skill growth is deliberate practice. But how much purposeful practice is necessary to achieve your goal? It may take 10,000 hours of concentrated training to achieve world-class expertise, but it usually takes far less time to become proficient enough for your own needs. You only need to learn a new skill that applies to you, and you don't need to become an expert in every skill.

Let's define a term called *rapid skill acquisition*. Rapid skill acquisition is the process of learning a skill in far less time than mastering a skill. It involves breaking the skill into small chunks, determining which of those components is the most crucial, learning everything necessary about that skill, and then diving into it and practicing.

The secret to quickly picking up new skills is to embrace the idea of sufficiency. Instead of discussing world-class competence in this book, we'll discuss building capacity. Leave the 10,000 hours to the experts. Twenty hours of focused, deliberate, and intense effort will be your starting point. You'll want to achieve your outcomes with a little effort, so you will get the things you want much faster. If you start with twenty hours of quick skill learning, you will have a greater chance of succeeding if you ultimately decide to master the talent. You will advance more rapidly and consistently and become an expert in record time by knowing what you are getting into and building the proper training schedule. Rapid skill development involves four main steps.

Step 1: Deconstruct the Skill

Divide the skill you want to learn into easily manageable subskills.

Step 2: Learn About the Skill

Gain sufficient knowledge of each subskill to enable sensible practice and to self-correct during practice.

Step 3: Remove Barriers

Remove any obstacles that get in the way of practicing a skill. Deal with all the emotional, physical, or societal barriers.

Step 4: Practice the Skill

Spend at least twenty hours refining the most crucial subskill.

Rapid skill development is not a complicated matter. Simply choose something to practice, decide how to practice it effectively, assign time, and keep practicing until you attain your desired performance level. No magic is involved. All it takes is intelligence and the purposeful effort put into a cause you care about. You can learn new abilities more quickly and with less effort with some preparation. That does not imply that the outcomes will be immediate. One of the main factors preventing people from learning new skills rapidly is the need for instant results. Rapid skill development isn't that quick. "Rapid" refers to learning a skill in a significantly shorter time than it would ordinarily take if you approached the process incorrectly.

I am very good at many sports, but I was not always like this. When I was in school, I was a shy student and always wanted to stay away from the spotlight. Even though I wanted to play with my fellows, I was terrified by the idea of being noticed. One reason was that I dreaded failure and felt that I would be greatly embarrassed if I failed in front of people. So I never participated in any sports and stayed away from the crowd. When I was admitted to college, I found that there was table tennis in my department, and my friends played there. I looked at them and wondered how they had such a grip on their hand movements and how they were so synchronized with their eyes. Once one of my friends, Oliver, offered for me to play with him, and I took the racket to try it. After a few shots, I was highly embarrassed and gave him back the racket. Many of my classmates were there, and they saw how incompetent I was. At that time, I told myself that playing any sport was not my cup of tea, and there was no need to embarrass myself in front of people.

The next day, Oliver offered for me to play again, but I refused. He insisted I play with him, but I was so discouraged that I didn't want to take the racket in my hand again. He offered to teach me how to play, but I told him, "I was never meant to play any sport. I am simply not capable of it. I don't even know how to hold a racket in my hand, let alone play proficiently. I am not a kid anymore; people judge me for how I am incapable of playing a sport." At that point, Oliver went quiet for a moment, then he said, "Okay, fine, then we will play after college hours so that there is no one here to judge you. Are you okay with that?" That sounded good because I didn't want to refuse my dear friend again.

Oliver was a pro player. He had been playing table tennis since childhood. He taught me how to hold the racket and hit the ping-pong ball. We played daily for one hour after our classes were over. Soon, I found it a fun sport and started to excel in it. I was amazed by my progress. After one month, I was confident enough to play in front of my other classmates, and at the end of college, I was one of the best table tennis players in my college.

Playing table tennis gave me confidence, which I lacked before. It completely changed my perspective on learning the sport, or any skill. Soon, I started thinking of learning other sports. I learned badminton, squash, golf, and snooker. I never played these games in a team to compete at college or university levels. I just learned these sports to add positive leisure activities to my life. Now I am a member of a sports club in my area, and I often go there to play these sports and to feel confident about myself.

I consider that time my turning point, as it completely changed the way I thought. When I entered professional life, I realized I needed to learn soft skills to excel among my competitors. Instead of giving myself lame excuses to avoid learning those things during my studies, I challenged myself to learn those skills to a level that gave me a good edge in my job. I experimented with these skills for a while, and as a result, my abilities grew exponentially.

If you systematically tackle a subject, you could also become proficient in many talents in less time. You might become close to the general level of competency in a month if you approach the practice of these abilities wisely. The time it takes you to learn a new talent mostly depends on how much focused time you are willing to devote to purposeful practice and intelligent experimenting, as well as how proficient you must become to reach the level you want.

Don't anticipate outcomes right away. Expect that the overall amount of time you spend will be far less than it would be if you started the process without a plan. Before delving deeper into the process, you should know that it has nothing to do with how you learned in school. Rapid skill acquisition is an entirely different process. Academic learning and skill development have almost no overlap with each other, let alone achieving it quickly.

LEARNING VS. ACQUIRING SKILLS

I studied a lot about French in school. I learned countless vocabulary words and grammatical rules. I memorized all of this information well enough to ace the exams. However, those tests had little to do with my ability to practice comprehending and speaking French practically or when communicating with a native speaker.

If I wanted to speak French well, a few weeks of trying to communicate with others in that language would have been more effective than four years of formal education. I didn't set out to become a fluent French speaker then. All I wanted was to pass the exam. Skill acquisition is learning a language so you can communicate with others. It entails putting what matters into practice, such as speaking French to others.

I am not saying that educating yourself on the skill you are trying to acquire is not essential; learning can be significant for understanding the skill and its related concepts. You can self-edit or self-correct while practicing a skill if you are familiar with related concepts. Knowing how to conjugate verbs in French will help you self-correct your speech more effectively when conversing with a native speaker. Learning common vocabulary words will improve your comprehension of what a native speaker is saying and help you remember the right words or phrases when in need. Learning aids planning, editing, and self-correction during practice. The issue arises when learning is confused with skill development. You must practice a new skill in a real-world setting if you want to master it. Learning improves practice, but it does not take its place. Learning alone is insufficient if performance is what matters.

TRAINING VS. ACQUIRING SKILLS

Additionally, there is a significant distinction between training and acquiring a skill. In this sense, training refers to using repetition to refine a talent that you have previously learned. If you want to keep improving, training is what you do once you have learned about the fundamental skill.

Training comes after skill acquisition. Training is the process of exerting yourself and growing. You get stronger as you train more. Training cannot be carried out or used effectively without a certain level of skill acquisition. Training and learning will undoubtedly make it simpler to become efficient, but they are not equivalent to skill acquisition. Some types of skill learning can be facilitated by preparation, but practice is always required. It's just like internships after graduation and before getting into practical life; the training gives you some formal ethics and know-how about the working environment. Training for any skill helps you to excel in that skill after you have acquired it.

For example, maybe you want to learn a specific programming language, so you enroll in a course. After the course, you feel that you have a lot of knowledge about the language and running its programs. You go to different companies for jobs, but they are not willing to hire you because they ask you how you will apply programming in real-life challenges and what offers you have for the customers of this software house. You never learned this during your course, so you decide to get an internship to gain practical insight into this field. You learn about different programming tools, maintaining a computer system, creating a program that is practically helpful for people, creating prototypes, and more.

So you learned the skill when you enrolled in the course. You acquired the skill by understanding it and running your own programs. You got trained in a skill for a competitive environment around you by joining the internship program.

FORMAL EDUCATION VS. ACQUIRING SKILLS

Despite the good intentions of scholars and educators worldwide, skill acquisition has very little to do with conventional schooling and certifications. Practice is necessary for the development of a skill. Extensive periods of prolonged, intense concentration are required. It calls for imagination, adaptability, and the freedom to establish your criteria for success. Regrettably, intensive training and certification might actively impede the development of new skills. Degree programs might be more detrimental than beneficial if the criteria to get the certificate are so burdensome that they prevent you from spending time practicing the necessary skills.

For example, a fashion design student aims to build a fashion store, so they enroll in a four-year fashion degree, which shows them how to polish their design aesthetics and how to use Adobe Illustrator to play with colors and designs to create new patterns. But when they enter the fashion-design market, they find that establishing their business is far more than designing on Illustrator.

So is there a connection between launching a business and earning a degree? Sure. The emphasis is on satisfying the standards, which take up most of the effort to acquire certification. Whether or not those requirements truly assist you in developing the abilities required to function in the real world remains a secondary concern.

TEN PRINCIPLES OF RAPID SKILL ACQUISITION

To rapidly acquire a particular skill, you must devise a proper strategy to achieve more in less time and with less effort. I have compiled some principles that will help you in rapid skill acquisition. These guidelines can help you develop a "temporary passion," in my opinion. Rapid skill learning happens automatically when you are so interested in something that other concerns temporarily fade. Consider these guidelines as a technique to pinpoint a skill that merits a brief obsession, concentrate on it, and eliminate any obstacles that prevent you from practicing it well. Many of these ideas may seem obvious to you, and that's fine. Keep in mind that understanding these principles will not be enough. To benefit from them, you must apply them.

1. PICK AN ENJOYABLE PROJECT

Would you like to invest your time in acquiring a skill that sounds boring to you? Even if you convince yourself for a while, you will soon realize you have made a horrible decision. Finding a problem, falling in love with it, and living life attempting to solve it are the best things to happen to a person. You can't go wrong with that method if you're looking for a strategy for leading a happy, fruitful life. Picking a fun activity is necessary for quick skill acquisition. You will acquire a skill more rapidly when you are more enthusiastic about learning the skill.

Finding a project that you love and that is your priority,

among other activities, is a very personal matter. For instance, you might not like learning many languages, but for me, it is fun to communicate in many ways. It also helps me connect with a broader audience. It has been a very long time since I have been interested in learning Spanish. It's a lovely language, and I adore the accents. I always wanted to speak like Spanish people and sing Spanish songs. As I am fond of this language and speaking Spanish sounds fun to me, I know it's a skill I will enjoy learning. I am purchasing Spanish classes in a few months, and I have a Spanish friend who has agreed to practice with me. I hope that it will be an incredible experience.

Things that interest you naturally stick in your mind longer than things you don't think much about. You'll learn far faster if you concentrate on mastering your top skill—your favorite project—before learning anything else.

2. CONCENTRATE YOUR EFFORTS ON ONE TALENT AT A TIME

One of the most common errors people make when learning new abilities is trying to pick up too many tasks simultaneously. However, learning new skills requires the devotion of time and attention. No skill will receive enough time and effort to produce noticeable improvement if you distribute your learning efforts across twenty different skills, and then only give half an hour per day to each skill.

Some people have a more challenging time ingraining this concept than others. I have always had a mentality that forces me to get involved in many things at once, and I constantly have hundreds of topics I want to learn more about. I find it emotionally challenging to choose to put off studying new information I come across or hear about. But I never learn anything when I try to work on various tasks simultaneously. Most of my time is spent jumping from one task to the other without gaining much progress in any particular task, and this results in frustration.

Pick just one skill you want to master. Put all your attention and effort into learning that talent, and temporarily put other skills on hold. I cannot stress this enough. Rapid skill learning requires concentrating on one key talent at a time. The different abilities are not permanently abandoned; instead, you are simply saving them for later.

3. ESTABLISH YOUR DESIRED PERFORMANCE LEVEL

A goal performance level is a straightforward statement that describes what perfection means to you, and which level you want to accomplish. How proficiently do you hope to be able to use the talent you are learning? Your optimal level of skill is your desired performance level. Consider it a concise summary of what you hope to accomplish and what you will be able to do once you have learned that skill. Your objective performance level should be as specific as possible. Setting a target performance level allows you to visualize what it would be like to perform at that level. It is simpler to figure out how to get there if you know how good you need to be or want to be. When a problem is expressed well, half of it is already resolved.

Depending on why you choose to learn the talent, you must determine your target performance level. If your goal is to have fun in your leisure time, you should aim for the task when you stop being frustrated and begin to enjoy the activity. What is the lowest standard of performance you will initially tolerate if you intend to start learning?

You can pause for a while when you reach your first target

level. The highest target performance levels are usually above a person's current capabilities, but are not impossible to reach. Generally speaking, the more flexible your target performance is, the quicker you can master the corresponding skill. If you have a world-class mastery mindset, doing this could seem unfair because, after all, you are merely lowering the bar to "win" more quickly.

Never forget that mastery at the highest level is not the goal of acquiring skills quickly. What you're aiming for isn't perfection, but ability and adequacy at maximum speed. It's crucial to remember that some competencies have safety requirements, which you should always consider when setting your target performance level. The goal is defeated if learning a new ability results in injury or death.

4. BREAK THE SKILL INTO SUBSKILLS

Most of the things that people consider to be skills are collections of subskills. After choosing a talent to concentrate on, the next step is to deconstruct it—to divide it into its component elements.

Finding the subskills that seem to be most significant is easier once the skill has been properly divided. You'll go forward faster and with less effort if you first concentrate on the essential subskills. Additionally, breaking down a skill makes it simpler to prevent feeling overpowered. It isn't possible to learn all aspects of a talent at once. Instead, it is more effective to concentrate on the subskills that offer the most spectacular overall rewards.

When you deconstruct the primary skill into its subskills, it becomes possible to identify the components of the skill that aren't important for amateur learners. By removing the low-priority subskills or approaches, you can devote more time and effort to acquiring the essential subskills.

5. ACQUIRE THE NECESSARY TOOLS

For exceptional practice and performance, most abilities require some prerequisites. It's challenging to learn how to fly a helicopter if you don't have access to one, just like playing tennis without a racket. What equipment, elements, and settings do you need to practice effectively? How do you find the best tools? Before beginning your practice, take a moment to list all the essential tools. You can maximize your practice time by ensuring you have the means to assist your learning.

6. REMOVE OBSTACLES TO PRACTICING

Various factors can hinder practice, making learning any skill much more challenging. These obstacles should be considered before practice begins, so they do not impede the session.

First, gather all the essential tools required for practicing so that you won't get distracted during practice sessions due to the unavailability of a tool. Do not rely on something not always available, like a particular instrument that can't be operated under certain conditions or for limited hours only.

Second, you should consider any doubt, fear, or embarrassment associated with that task. These emotional obstacles are sometimes extreme, and they can significantly decrease your progress.

These factors make it more challenging to begin practicing, reducing your acquisition speed. It is a losing tactic to rely entirely on willpower to fight these obstacles. People only have a certain amount of will each day, so you must be selective with how you apply it.

To use your willpower to help in skill acquisition, you

must invest your energies in learning a skill rather than wasting your energy dealing with obstacles. You will be more comfortable if you solve all the issues beforehand. You will acquire the skill faster if you rearrange your surroundings to make it as simple as possible to begin practicing.

7. INVEST TIME IN PRACTICING REGULARLY

You must assign an appropriate time to practice that skill regularly. Mastery doesn't come without practice. If you can't make time for practice today because you're too busy, make it tomorrow, then keep one thing in your mind: If you are not doing it today, you will not find time for it tomorrow. "Finding time for something" is a misconception; you always make time for your priorities. People frequently want to continue engaging in many of their favorite hobbies, such as playing games or watching TV, while resolving to learn a new skill. In this way, you are just deceiving yourself. You will never finish a task if you rely on finding the time to do it. You must create time if you want to do it.

You need to plan twenty-four hours of the day for this, just like students who make timetables for their school days. If you sleep seven to eight hours a day, you are still left with sixteen to seventeen hours, which are enough for proper planning. You might work for some of these hours, and there are some hours you want to give to your family. The time you have left over is what you can use to learn new skills. In a whole day, if you can assign two hours to your favorite skill that you are looking forward to learning, you will get the desired results with proper focus and concentration. More extensive devoted periods are preferable if you want to advance your abilities as rapidly as possible.

The ideal strategy for finding time for skill development is to decide which time-wasting activities to cut out. I suggest keeping a detailed diary of your daily activities as an experiment. You will be surprised by the findings of this timetable. If you make a few difficult decisions to eliminate time-wasting activities, you will have much more time for skill development. The more available time you have daily, the less overall time it will take to learn new abilities. I advise cutting out as much time-wasting as possible to allow at least 120 minutes of practice each day.

I also advise committing to practice for at least twenty hours combined. You must continue to practice after you begin, until you have put in these twenty hours. If you find yourself stuck somewhere, don't give up; you can't stop until you have put in twenty hours or reached your desired performance level.

The early stages of the skill-acquisition process typically feel more complex than they are. You will frequently feel puzzled and encounter unknown difficulties and roadblocks. Pre-committing to twenty hours makes resisting simpler than giving up when you experience even the smallest challenge. Think of this strategy as a test of your resilience: You would not let a minor problem prevent you from doing what you have determined you genuinely want to do. You will either find a solution or try your hardest for the next twenty hours.

8. BUILD QUICK FEEDBACK LOOPS

Quick feedback refers to receiving accurate performance evaluations as soon as possible. When it takes longer to receive feedback, it will take more time to master the ability. After breaking your skill into subskills, evaluate every step of progress toward your goal. Quickly assess yourself after each step and ask others for feedback so that you make timely decisions if there is any need to change the strategy.

Rapid skill acquisition is automatically facilitated by quick feedback. When you receive the feedback with little delay, it is far simpler to link any criticism to your activities and make the necessary modifications.

There are a lot of resources for helpful criticism. Skilled coaches and mentors often provide rapid feedback on how you are doing and if there is any need to make required adjustments. Along with relying on coaches and other people around you, you can also assess yourself quickly by using capture tools like video cameras. This is the era of technology, and you should make the most of it. AI assistants and other technology devices instantly let you know when you make a mistake. The quicker the feedback is that you incorporate into your practice, the more quickly you will master the skill.

9. PRACTICE IN SHORT, REGULAR SESSIONS

Brains are designed to learn—to identify patterns, experiment with different scenarios, and predict what will probably happen next. They aren't designed to calculate how much time has been invested performing a task or how long it will take to be done with accuracy.

It is incredibly simple to miscalculate your practice time when you have just started learning a new skill. Time tends to move more slowly, and it might seem like you have been training for longer when you are not good at something. Therefore, it's best to start with as little time as you can comfortably give to the task. Purchase a timer and set it for ten or fifteen minutes. When you are comfortable with this, you can increase the practice time. The only thing you have to do once the timer is set is continue to train until it expires, without making any excuses.

This straightforward method will make it simpler to continue practicing for extended periods of time, despite being weary or frustrated. The more sustained practice sessions you put in, the quicker you will pick up new skills. You will make significant progress in a relatively short time if you set aside time for three to five brief practice sessions each day.

10. PRIORITIZE SPEED AND QUALITY

It's tempting to concentrate on practicing flawlessly and quickly as you start to learn a new talent, but this can be frustrating when you cannot bring perfection to your work. This is why you first need to ensure the quality of your efforts, even if you are just investing a fraction of the time. But try increasing your speed to achieve more in less time as you gain momentum and perfection.

You'll learn the skill more quickly if you practice more frequently and promptly. This does not mean that when practicing, you should disregard the proper form. Some abilities necessitate a quality of form, especially those that call for physical actions or motions. Make sure your practice form is sufficient and meets your desired performance level. Increase the speed to facilitate faster skill acquisition once you are practicing with proper form.

IS IT EFFECTIVE?

Will using this approach speed up your skill acquisition? Yes. When people start practicing a new ability, their performance increases drastically in a relatively short time. Your abilities will naturally advance in a short time frame if you begin practicing something new. The key is to get practicing as soon as you can. Instead of thinking or planning about practicing, engage in actual practice.

Without practice, it is easy to feel like you are devoting a lot of time to a skill when you are wasting time dealing with obstacles. Dealing with obstacles is not equivalent to practicing a skill. You can invest years of mental and emotional energy into learning something you have wanted to study for a long time, but if you're reluctant to start, you won't become any better. You can squander just as much energy aimlessly wandering if you don't know where you are going or don't have a clear plan for getting there.

These ten guidelines are meant to assist you in getting rid of these viewpoints and assist in replacing them with actions essential to the skill-acquisition procedure.

You will learn a skill more rapidly if you put more time and effort into the first two stages of the process and less time into activities that don't advance your learning.

The ten principles I mentioned will not only let you acquire skills rapidly, but also make an energetic start to your learning journey. It is essential to focus on how you start any task, be it learning or anything else. Starting off well means you will be halfway to learning that skill. This is how powerful the starting point is. Applying the given criteria and principles to your current desired skill will make your practice more productive and efficient, accelerating your learning of the skill. These concepts are not complex. They involve applying common sense, planning, and preparation to a skill you want to develop—nothing more, nothing less.

CHAPTER 7
LEARNING EFFECTIVELY

 Tell me and I forget, teach me and I may remember, involve me and I learn.

BENJAMIN FRANKLIN

Effective learning refers to teaching and learning methods that actively aid learners in their academic development and personal improvement. It enables you to learn and use any knowledge or skill more rapidly, thoroughly, and effortlessly. Effective learning is useful in all situations, whether you are a student, a working person, or a homemaker.

If people actively participate in learning and discussion, they will more likely comprehend and remember what they're learning. When students take an active role in their learning, they can identify and define academic goals that will help them advance. They gain independence and ownership of their education and learning experience by establishing these goals. Active learning will assist you in determining what you anticipate from any knowledge or skill you wish to acquire and how you intend to use it in your daily life. Learning is considered successful or effective when the learning performance matches the desired learning outcome.

TEN PRINCIPLES OF EFFECTIVE LEARNING

As humans, we are always in a hurry. People want to achieve everything as quickly as possible, which includes acquiring a skill. But you must be patient and figure things out first. In this book, I have attempted to guide you on how you can learn anything faster and more effectively. But it doesn't mean you should skip the steps needed to acquire those skills. I have already discussed the importance of patience when learning something. I have also emphasized doing exercises, yoga, and meditation, because these things make the mind calm, patient, productive, and more focused. In this chapter, you will learn a few necessary principles for boosting your learning experience.

Learning skills is not the same as acquiring them. Before you start practicing something, you must actively learn it. It's an excellent idea to assess your current skill, and to assess where you stand to monitor your progress effectively. This helps you define your goals according to your needs and capacity and how you plan to achieve them. Effective learning gives you confidence, which is important for skill acquisition. It helps make you resilient when the practice session starts. Learning makes practicing more effective, allowing you to devote more practice time to refining the most crucial subskills first. You can save a lot of time, effort, and psychological burden by studying before you start practicing. To boost your learning performance, get an idea of how you can master the skill efficiently through smart learning with these ten principles of effective learning.

Although not all of these principles apply to every skill, you will discover that a number of them are applicable. Simply go through this checklist whenever you want to learn a new skill and choose which guidelines apply to your task.

1. RESEARCH THE SKILLS AND RELATED TOPICS

It's essential to research a field extensively before getting into it. This can make you aware of any unwanted situations that you might encounter in the future, and aware of how you can adequately manage everything beforehand. This is an era of technology, and if you are not using it well, you're wasting your life. Search on the web; you will get thousands of websites and books with information related to the skill you want to learn. Go to a bookstore and read the books on that skill, or look through the bookshelves at a nearby library for materials essential to the skill.

Find at least two books, a few authentic websites, courses, instructional DVDs, or other materials that are related to the skill you are attempting to learn.

Note that you don't need to spend hours remembering these materials. But you also need to know that watching or reading is not time spent practicing. You aren't studying for a test. This preliminary research aims to quickly identify the most crucial subskills, essential elements, and necessary instruments for practice. If you have more information about the talent beforehand, you will be more prepared to start. Gathering significant information on the subject is vital to creating a thorough picture of skill development.

Skimming is preferable to deep reading for quick skill acquisition. You can trust the truth of the patterns you detect and arrange your practice accordingly by noting ideas and techniques that repeatedly appear in different literature. If you want to play an instrument, read good books on musical instruments. Make yourself familiar with all the basics of any skill you are looking for. Instead of starting from scratch, you might use approaches that have been refined through the years by experts in that field.

If a method or procedure is discussed in several different resources, there's a significant chance it will help you become an expert in any area. You can try the strategies you think will be most helpful in your situation once you have discovered them, saving you tons of time-consuming trial and error methods.

2. OVERCOME YOUR LIMITATIONS BY DIVING IN

Many people, after doing research, become confused about a few things related to training or practicing a particular skill. Sometimes, they start doubting their ability to learn that talent because many things seem out of their reach. Thus, it becomes easy to lose interest in learning. But the human brain can do wonders. Be confident in yourself while trying to learn. Getting confused about a few things before practicing anything is typical.

There are many things related to that skill you might not be familiar with. You will come across certain concepts, methods, and ideas in the early research that you don't fully comprehend. You will observe practitioners performing things you don't understand and read phrases you don't know. But there is no need to worry. Your initial perplexity is very acceptable. In fact, it is excellent that you are heading into the chaos. Even if you don't initially comprehend many things associated with the skill, everything will start to make sense once you start practicing.

Once you get some experience, the same confusion will start to dissipate. You need to understand that solving confusion is itself a type of clarity. It's crucial to understand your confusion level. Knowing precisely why you are confused identifies your concerns, which helps you determine what you need to investigate or do next to clear up your confusion. If you are not perplexed by your initial research, you are not learning as quickly as you need to.

You are on the right track if you begin to feel intimidated or uneasy about the pace you are attempting. The more baffled you are at first, the more pressure you will feel to sort things out. It will help you learn faster and work harder to become more productive toward the project. The biggest emotional obstacle to learning new skills is a lack of willingness to take risks. Once you become confident in yourself and take the risk, everything will start to make its way to you. Gaining confidence and telling yourself repeatedly that you will master the skill with practice will help you remove any previous misconceptions about the skill.

3. IDENTIFY MENTAL MODELS AND HOOKS

A general term for any idea, concept, or vision you keep in your brain is a *mental model*. People's overall understanding of the world is based on these mental models. They influence not only the way people understand and think, but also how they perceive connections and opportunities. Mental models help people to analyze things, minimize complexity, and determine why some things are more important than others.

Natural patterns, ideas, and methods that repeatedly

appear will become apparent as you investigate. The most fundamental learning tool is the cognitive model, a technique to comprehend and name an actual object or connection in the real world. As you build more precise mental models, predicting what will happen when you do something will become simpler.

Additionally, mental models influence how you think and act. They are the methods of thought you employ to comprehend reality, reach conclusions, and address issues. Learning a new mental model can change how you perceive the world. Your mental models and their applicability to the topic at hand determine the caliber of your reasoning. You are more likely to have the appropriate models to see reality if you are familiar with more models, and thus you will have access to a more extensive toolbox. It seems that variety is essential when it comes to enhancing your capacity for decision-making. Therefore, multiple mental models will give you many options to choose from, to make the best decisions possible.

Mental models make it easier to convey your thoughts and share your experiences with others. You can better understand life by using various mental models. Here are a few examples:

- Supply and demand is one mental model that can help you comprehend how the economy functions.
- Entropy is a mental model in which you may visualize disorder and decay in nature.
- The mental model of Occam's razor states that instead of wasting time trying to debunk complex scenarios, you can make more confident decisions

by relying on the explanation with the fewest moving components.

- A game-theory mental model can help you comprehend how alliances and trust work.
- Another famous model is the evolution model, in which nature decides which species should evolve according to changing conditions and which species will be extinct soon.

These mental models have facilitated people's comprehension of numerous concepts and formulated strategies according to their situations. So devise a mental model that best suits your needs and is effective for your learning. These models will guide you throughout your practicing and learning sessions. The more mental models you can discover during your preliminary research, the simpler it will be to apply them throughout the practicing period.

4. CONSIDER THE WORST CASE SCENARIO

It's nice when everyone has an optimistic approach toward things. But when you are in the planning phase, it is better to look for pitfalls. Instead of just focusing on success, look for loopholes and circumstances you may encounter in the future. What if you experienced the worst-case scenario? How would you face that? Is there any plan to deal with that situation? What kind of loss would you expect through it?

Thinking in this way doesn't make you pessimistic. Instead, it makes you aware of all the possible outcomes and helps you deal with the unwanted situation in a better way. It sounds paradoxical, but thinking about failure rather than success can help you understand a new skill. Inversion is a method of problem-solving that can be used to learn the fundamentals of almost anything. You'll be able to see important aspects that aren't immediately obvious by considering the worst-case scenario.

Let's say you and your friends have organized a hiking trip. You select your outfit, look for the comfiest shoes with decent grip, put on your sunglasses, and sing as you get ready. Everything appears to be going according to plan, but have you considered any unfavorable circumstances? Is it safe to visit that location? What if you encounter a wild animal while hiking? What if one of your friends faints while you're climbing? What if you get lost in the mountains with no mobile service to call for help?

These thoughts sound depressing, but they are helpful because they highlight strategies that could save lives in such circumstances.

You should first ask people in the area if that place is safe. Has anyone reported any kind of crime or encountered a wild animal? Plan your trip according to the guidelines given by these local guides. Take a first aid kit to handle minor injuries or medical conditions. Take a lot of water with you to stay hydrated during exertion.

You are good to go if you are already familiar with the hiking path. These thoughts will aid you in updating your shopping list. You will consider packing a basic first aid kit, water bottles, sunscreen, a flashlight, or any other item you might need in an emergency, in addition to your clothing, shoes, and sunglasses.

5. HAVE A DISCUSSION WITH PRACTITIONERS TO SET A GOAL

Early education supports the formation of realistic expectations about how a beginner should start practicing. It is common to underestimate the difficulty level of mastering a new skill. Sometimes, people think it is easy to do a particular task. However, they only face reality once beginning practice. Therefore, it is always a good idea to address these expectations at the start by getting help from professionals.

Enroll in a few relevant courses for the skill you want to practice. This will help you get professional guidelines and familiarize you with various terms associated with that skill. An experienced person will help you establish realistic goals and determine your best practice route.

Before you spend your time and effort learning a skill, it will be helpful to clear up any misunderstandings and misconceptions by speaking to those who have already mastered the talent. Maintaining your interest in the practice and avoiding being discouraged will be much simpler if you know what to expect as you advance.

6. ELIMINATE DISTRACTIONS

The primary foe of learning anything is distractions. Rapid skill acquisition slows down or becomes impossible in the presence of distractions. Lack of focused practice is equivalent to doing nothing, and it results in delayed or nonexistent skill improvement.

It's discouraging to invest your time and effort into something without seeing any results. This occurs mostly due to distractions. Distractions waste not just your valuable time, but also your concentrated practice. You can avoid losing time and energy by reducing as many distractions as possible before you begin training.

Electronic and biological sources are among the most common daily distractions. Electronic distractions include phones, the Internet, television, and other gadgets on which people have become dependent. Turn them off or remove them from your surroundings if they aren't required for practice. However, if you are practicing for something that requires your smartphone, then focus yourself only on learning by disabling all other unnecessary apps and putting your phone on airplane mode. This is quite helpful while practicing. The rest of the responsibility is yours and depends on how honest you are with yourself while practicing so that you don't switch between apps.

Sometimes, it can be even more challenging to deal with biological distractions. Pets, coworkers, friends, and family can all be biological distractions. They cannot be turned off or put on silent. It is better to give specific times to these relations, and then ask them to cooperate with you during your learning period. This may increase the likelihood that they will respect your practice time, since you cooperated with them when they were looking for you. With fewer interruptions while training, you'll acquire the skill faster.

7. USE SPACED REPETITION AND REINFORCEMENT TO MEMORIZE

To apply what you have learned while practicing, you must be able to recall related ideas rapidly. After learning, take a break and then recall what you have learned. You can do it multiple times, which will help you assess how much you retain after each practice session. Moreover, this repetition engraves the information you have learned in your mind and improves your memory.

Memorization is a necessary component of many skills. Your memory, however, is not always reliable. When you learn anything new, unless you repeat the idea within a particular time frame, you will pretty much forget it. Repetition strengthens the concept and aids in its consolidation into long-term memory. Memory follows an exponential decay curve, so you tend to forget the content at a very high rate when there is no reinforcement. Fresh concepts need to be reinforced frequently, but as you become more familiar with a topic or skill, you need to review it less regularly to memorize it precisely.

By using the memorization approach of spaced repetition and reinforcement, you can regularly and methodically examine fundamental ideas and facts. It is always a good idea to revisit and revise challenging topics more frequently. In contrast, less complicated topics and those with which you are already familiar can be changed less regularly as they are already embedded in your memory. Spaced repetition and reinforcement are relatively easy to do with the help of flash cards or flash card software. Once you make them, it simply takes a few minutes every day to go over your flash cards. These systems can speed up the learning process for new concepts, methods, and procedures by systematizing the review procedure and monitoring recalls. If you frequently study the cards, you will quickly memorize the relevant principles and ideas.

It is vital to remember that developing skills typically requires far more effort than learning academic material. You don't need more than spaced repetition if your main goal is memorizing concepts, ideas, or language to pass an exam. This method works best in situations where quick knowledge recall is crucial. Spaced repetition and reinforcement are beneficial for learning common vocabulary words of a new language. You are usually better off avoiding flash cards when quick recall isn't essential, and instead should make the most of your practice and experimenting time.

8. CREATE CHECKLISTS TO TRACK YOUR PERFORMANCE

Routines involve actions you do effortlessly every day, such as getting up from bed in the morning, exercising, preparing coffee, managing your documents, or packing. However, there is always room for improvement. Sometimes you forget things, or things seem to be mismanaged, especially when trying to learn something new or fix something in your routine. Modifying your routine is the best method to guarantee that these crucial components occur with the least amount of additional effort. Keep a diary and make a checklist for recalling requirements for each practice session. This is a method of systematizing the procedure, which liberates your attention so you can concentrate on more crucial issues. If you're someone who constantly complains about memory problems and forgetfulness, try this checklist strategy. Write down what your goals are today, what you have learned today, and what is still pending on your list. It helps a lot. It helps you remember everything and avoid getting into trouble.

Mockups are tools that make sure you always approach a skill in the same way. Mockups are helpful when preparing for a real-world competition or when you must perform in front of an audience. They allow you to rehearse in a situation that closely resembles the real event. When you succeed in a mockup, your confidence grows, helping you to do well in the actual performance. Your practice will be more effective if you create mockups and checklists. Additionally, they facilitate visualization during training, benefiting you from the mental rehearsal.

9. EXPERIMENT WITH DIFFERENT THINGS

Learning new skills includes experimentation or trying new things to discover if they work for you or not. Every idea and method does not work well for everyone. It is good to follow an expert in that field, but sometimes, your inner self guides you better than others. When you start practicing, look for things that do not work out for you the way they work for others. Then experiment with alternatives, and find what is best for you. Here is a scientific method:

- **Observations:** Observe your level of skill acquisition and identify your weak areas.
- **Knowns:** Identify your preliminary knowledge about the topic or skill you are working on.
- **Hypotheses:** What experiment do you want to devise that you think will help you improve yourself?
- **Tests:** Figure out how that test will be performed.
- **Predictions:** What are the expected outcomes that you predict after experimentation?

Use a notebook or other reference material to keep track of your experiments and develop hypotheses as you practice. You could design more effective experiments to test your hypotheses if you keep track of your expectations and develop new possibilities. Since this will also keep track of what you have already tried, you won't need to waste your time on that technique anymore if it does not work for you.

10. RESPECT YOUR BIOLOGICAL NEEDS

Your body and brain are biological systems with biological demands such as nutrition, hydration, movement, rest, and sleep. It is pretty easy to exert excessive pressure on yourself to achieve something, but that is sometimes detrimental to your health. Without the proper inputs, your body and mind won't produce effective output. When expecting good performance, you need to provide for your body's biological needs. Do not exert your body too much—you cannot practice all day long. Approximately ninety minutes of intense concentration per learning cycle is an ideal amount of time. Any longer and your body and mind will become exhausted and need a break.

Take frequent breaks between practice sessions. Use that time to relax, eat, talk to someone, have a snack, take a nap, or do something else. This will make you feel refreshed and ready for the next practice session. This idea will complement your practice and enhance your skill. Practice in small sessions and set a goal for each session. After each session, relax while preparing your mind for the upcoming session. If necessary, you can divide your practice time into smaller segments and take a quick break in the middle, such as twenty minutes of practice followed by a ten-minute rest. That will be pretty helpful, and you will not lose your stamina while practicing.

FEYNMAN'S METHOD FOR EFFECTIVE LEARNING

Richard Feynman (1918-1988) was a Nobel Prize-winning physicist and one of the most famous scientists of the 20th century. He contributed significantly to the development of quantum mechanics, particle physics, and the theory of quantum electrodynamics. Feynman was also known for his exceptional ability to explain complex scientific concepts in a simple and engaging way.

The Feynman technique is a learning strategy that maximizes your potential and compels you to understand a subject thoroughly. The Feynman technique is based on the principle that if you want to comprehend anything completely, you should describe it in simple terms. The Feynman method of teaching and communicating is a mental model for delivering information with compact ideas and straightforward language. This strategy can help you acquire new ideas more quickly, fill in knowledge gaps, retain information, or study more effectively.

HOW TO APPLY THE FEYNMAN TECHNIQUE

The Feynman technique consists of four main steps.

Step 1: Choose a Subject

Identify the topic that you want to learn. Take a piece of paper, and at the top, write the name of the concept you are learning. Now gather information on that topic from different sources and list all your knowledge about the subject. Add new information to the notes if you find further information.

Step 2: Teach a Child

You're far ahead of the game if you can teach an idea to a child. Concentrate on utilizing straightforward language. Don't restrict your explanation to a summary or a single definition; instead, push yourself to think through a few examples to make sure you can apply the idea. First, write the subject matter you wish to teach on a blank piece of paper. Then include all of your knowledge about that subject beneath that topic. However, the secret is to write it clearly and precisely so that a child can comprehend what you're saying.

Step 3: Determine Your Weak Areas

Primary learning takes place at this stage. Examine your explanation and note any points where you think you're missing information or that your justification is tenuous. After identifying weaknesses, review the relevant literature, your records, or any examples you can find to help you better comprehend them. You'll benefit from highlighting knowledge gaps when you compile and arrange your notes into a coherent story. When someone challenges your knowledge of the subject, you can refer them to your sources. Go to the books if you don't know something. Return to the source and gather details that will permit you to fill in the gaps.

Step 4: Review, Organize, Simplify, and Finalize

Rephrase any sections of your explanation that have a lot of technical jargon or complex terminology into simpler words. Verify that your statement could make sense to someone who lacks background knowledge. Put your notes together and start to tell a story with clear explanations. Begin by learning the fundamentals to understand the topic entirely. Read your narrative aloud a few times. Imagine telling the tale to a group of pupils in a classroom. You can then hear where language becomes complex. To improve your comprehension of the story, use analogies and short words.

Using this trick can help you stay out of people's traps.

The next time you listen to someone using jargon or complex terms, ask them to explain things in simple words. If they manage to explain it in simpler terms, it means they fully grasp the content. If they become restless, they don't fully comprehend what they're saying.

SYNTOPIC READING FOR EFFECTIVE LEARNING

This method emphasizes reading widely across a body of literature and is more concerned with synthesis than analysis. By recontextualizing the author's work in light of the reader's theories and evolving ideas, the reader seeks to "bring the author to terms" rather than merely "coming to terms" with the work. This is equivalent to profoundly understanding the conceptual framework.

FOUR LEVELS OF READING

There are four reading levels, each getting harder and more sophisticated as you advance.

Elementary reading: You can read and understand a page at that point. I refer to it as "basic" reading. This is a purely mechanical interpretation of the text and an understanding of the literal meaning of the symbols.

Inspectional reading: This is a quick overview of the book's layout and primary ideas. It seeks to comprehend the book as fully as possible in a constrained time. This is accomplished by reading the glossary, table of contents, and essential chapter summaries.

Analytical reading: This seeks to comprehend the book as fully as possible. You should not only try to understand what is being said, but also form a judgment about its authenticity. You work hard as a demanding reader. It necessitates that you approach a text with specific questions and take notes in a particular method.

Syntopical reading: This is the most challenging and elevated form of reading. It includes modeling dialogues between authors and comparing books and authors to one another.

HOW DOES SYNTOPIC READING WORK?

Reading syntopically, which employs analytical skills across various texts, is considered the most difficult of all reading styles. The concept of syntopic reading was introduced fifty years ago by Mortimer Adler and Charles Van Doren. They believed that the ultimate purpose of being well-read was to have the ability to think critically.

Consider reading to be a lifetime journey of discovery. As you proceed down this route, you quickly learn that there are conflicting views on every vital issue. Divergent points of view, for an intelligent reader, produce tension that calls for the next step in resolution. Reading syntopically offers a fresh perspective and a quick way to combine many points of view.

Good readers comprehend all sides of a subject and draw

their own opinions. Reading systematically ensures that more of your concepts are derived from your thoughts. This is accomplished by exposing yourself to many points of view before selecting or creating one that finally resonates with you. Your reasoning, general knowledge, and reflection on experience all contribute to your reality, not just the most recent book you read. To grasp something better, you usually need to read numerous books about it.

Reading syntopically involves two stages. Let's discuss them briefly.

Getting ready phase: You put together a bibliography while you're preparing. You must thoroughly analyze the subject and list every one of them for yourself. The next step is to determine which books from that collection will be helpful to you and appropriate for your practice session.

Reading phase: Within the bibliography, find the most noteworthy texts. Bring the authors to an agreement. Create a list of inquiries that most authors could answer. Define the issues by arranging the writers' conflicting responses. Arrange the questions and topics to comprehend them as easily as possible.

For whatever goal you are pursuing, syntopic reading aims to understand an entire field, subject, argument, or expertise. To display sufficient performance, it is critical to use actual quotations from the writers as support for your posed challenges and from the concerns they address.

CHAPTER 8
DIFFERENT LEARNING APPROACHES

A learning approach is any strategy you employ to acquire knowledge. The primary goal is to categorize learning strategies based on the goals they help to achieve. Therefore, if a learning strategy aids memorization, it will be defined entirely in terms of this attribute rather than how the brain functions, how information is maintained, or by any other scientific theory. It is entirely up to you to choose a teaching strategy that complements your learning objectives. This ensures that the process works as intended. Regardless of the learner's preferred learning style, each method of instruction is most effective for achieving the intended goal.

It may feel as though teaching and learning are routine tasks. It is often assumed that everyone in school learns the same things. But in reality, that's not the case. Because everyone's learning capacity differs and the teaching styles of the instructors vary, not everyone learns the same things in school. Instead, it depends on the teachers' and students' learning approaches, which determines how much the students learn. The art and science of teaching are addressed from various educational perspectives. Many of them were invented by educational theorists who researched learning science to ascertain what and for whom it is most effective.

Individuals at the early stages of learning do not recognize the importance of education and its impact later in their lives. Most of the time, their main goal is to ace an upcoming exam. So they prefer a surface approach where they concentrate more on memorizing facts for a test or exam rather than actually understanding them.

People should be guided appropriately, and their insight should be modified by encouraging them to set lifetime goals instead of just focusing on the coming exam. When their mindset is changed, they start to learn in different ways, taking a deep approach to learning and striving to understand the content rather than just memorizing it. However, learning is not only associated with classrooms and kids, as we have already discussed in detail; it is a whole lifestyle. Therefore, devising proper strategies and approaches from early years helps in lifetime learning.

Socrates, Plato, and Aristotle were among the first Greek philosophers to express interest in how people learn, although formal theories about education were not devised until the early twentieth century. These philosophers investigated whether knowledge and truth might be discovered either internally or by observation of the outside world. Psychologists started using empirical research to provide an answer to this query in the nineteenth century. The intention was to design teaching strategies aligned with an objective understanding of how individuals learn. The primary purpose of developing these strategies was to make learning fast and a pleasant experience for everyone. It helps more people learn and enhance their understanding of everything around them. It also gives a chance to everyone, even unprivileged people. Once you learn proper strategies and use the right approach to learning, you will see doors of limitlessness open to you.

The conflict between behaviorist theory and cognitive psychology was discussed among educational theorists in the twentieth century. Numerous ideas have been developed over time to investigate the steps in the learning process. The majority of learning theories focus on the importance of imparting learning.

Despite the diversity of learning strategies, there are three primary schools of thought: behaviorist, cognitive constructivist, and social constructivist. I'll give a quick overview of each form of learning theory here.

BEHAVIORIST APPROACH

Even if you are only a bit familiar with learning behaviors, you will understand this strategy very quickly. As the name implies, this strategy focuses primarily on behavior. This method works best for learning anything that intends to alter behavior. Several talents necessitate a shift in behavior as opposed to information retention.

This approach is mainly employed in practical education. It was presented by B. F. Skinner. It predicts that environmental factors cause learning to occur. The learning facilitator's job is to present essential and relevant stimuli for the learner to react to and gain the necessary background or expertise. The foundation of the behaviorist approach to learning is that proper behavior can be taught by repeatedly doing a task and receiving feedback from the facilitator. Positive feedback stimulates and reinforces accomplishment, while negative feedback and prompt correction discourage the repetition of a mistake or bad behavior.

By providing reinforcement, the link between stimuli and reaction can be strengthened. There are both good and adverse effects of reinforcement. Anything that makes the desired response stronger is a positive reinforcer. In training, where learning is the goal, vocal praise, a good grade, or a sense of accomplishment may boost this and encourage the learner. Conversely, if verbal praise is withheld, this will have a negative impact and cause lower enthusiasm to learn. The method also predicts that there is only one correct path, only one truth that students need to acquire, and that knowledge is universal for all students. This is why it strongly focuses on teacher or trainer control; trainers use external reinforcement to inspire and motivate learners to meet predetermined goals.

Anything involving behavior can be taught using this method. Enhance your emotional stability, work on controlling your anger, or learn other self-help techniques. Repetition and reinforcement are vital components of the behavioristic learning strategy.

COGNITIVE APPROACH

Behaviorist learning theories strongly emphasize the tutor being assertive and the passive learner not having much choice but to behave in a preset way. In contrast, cognitive approaches focus on how the active mind processes learning opportunities and develops. The term *cognition* refers to the mental processes of the brain's capacity to take in and retain the knowledge gained through experience and senses. A Swiss psychologist, Jean Piaget, the father of cognitive learning theory, advocated for a learner-centered approach to education. He claimed that learning depends on adaptation, assimilation, and stability. Piaget believed that learning is the act of connecting new knowledge to what people already know. To facilitate this, the teacher should create a comfortable learning environment, a setting that fosters learners' curiosity and values their insights.

The following are key characteristics of cognitive learning.

1. Comprehension

For cognitive learning to be effective and advantageous to you, understand the primary purpose for why you are learning a certain subject.

2. Memory

The unproductive practice of cramming material is discouraged by cognitive learning. Your capacity to connect new knowledge to experiences or information from the past is enhanced when you have a good memory and thorough comprehension of the subject.

3. Implementation

You can use newly learned knowledge or abilities in real-world settings by using cognitive learning methodologies.

They support you as you work to improve your problem-solving abilities.

Memorization and retention are the main goals of the cognitive learning approach. Do not interpret this as a method of information cramming. Instead, it uses a deep system that enables the brain to comprehend and retain the data. It is an excellent learning method for anything that requires memorizing larger chunks of material. However, you also want to ensure you fully comprehend all the information ingrained in your mind. This method is excellent for research because it focuses on memory-intensive activities.

The following is a summary of two prominent classical cognitive philosophers.

JOHN DEWEY

According to Dewey, learning entails "learning to think." To him, learning involves more than just carrying out a task or activity; it also entails reflection and learning from it. He believed the goal of thought was to reach a state of equilibrium, which allows a person to solve difficulties and get them ready for more research.

Dewey, who is frequently connected with "progressive education," opposed traditional systems of teaching that place the student in a passive role while reinforcing information in their minds. He argued that this style of learning is superficial. According to him, learning only happens when the learner actively participates in the activity. The learner must be able to reflect on the material offered for effective learning; they must be ready to "experience" the information, and the best method to do this is to use prior knowledge. Therefore, it may be said that Dewey was a leading advocate of active learning.

Dewey's approach to learning places a greater emphasis on the function of teachers and trainers in learners' growth than the behaviorist model, albeit more indirectly. Planning sessions that promote discussion of the presented information and reflective thinking, for instance, will foster an environment where learners can organize their learning.

B.S. BLOOM

Bloom, a different cognitive approach thinker, believed that learning took place in the "affective domain" and that thoughts and feelings affect the outcome of learning. It also affects the "cognitive domain" related to memory and comprehension. According to Bloom, simultaneous learning between the cognitive and emotive domains occurs cumulatively depending on the difficulty level. Individual differences will determine how each student uses the cognitive and emotional realms.

Bloom's taxonomy was another significant contribution to the teaching and learning process. Bloom's taxonomy is a hierarchical classification of cognitive abilities that support teacher instruction and student learning. It is a classification system for the many goals and competencies that teachers set for their students. The following six degrees of learning are included in Bloom's taxonomy, which was recently modified. You can structure your course's learning objectives, modules, and assessments using these six levels.

Remembering: This step includes obtaining, identifying, and retrieving important information from long-term memory. Examples include memorizing a poem or recalling mathematical formulas.

Understanding: This step includes understanding oral, textual, or visual material relevant to the subject and then interpreting, classifying, or summarizing. Examples include classifying animals according to their classes or summarizing the events of a short novel.

Applying: This step includes performing, developing, or using appropriate execution techniques. Examples of activities include utilizing a formula to solve an issue, choosing a layout to achieve a goal, or retracing the steps taken to enact a new law through a particular government or system.

Analyzing: This step includes separating a piece of information into its component pieces and figuring out how those parts connect to one another and to a larger structure or goal by distinguishing, organizing, and attributing. Examples for the level of analysis include describing how the phases of the scientific method work, listing the components of democracy, or explaining why a device isn't working.

Evaluating: This step includes making decisions based on parameters and standards by examining and evaluating. Examples include making a decision regarding an ethical conundrum or interpreting the significance of a specific physical law.

Creating: This step includes combining pieces to create cohesive or useful information or rearranging elements into a different pattern via planning or production. Examples of creation-level activities include creating a fresh approach to an "old" issue while reorganizing, or writing a poem based on a predetermined theme and tone.

HUMANIST APPROACH

The humanism learning theory, developed by Abraham Maslow, focuses on the growth of students. The idea of kindness for all serves as the cornerstone of humanistic theory. It aspires for a peaceful, united world in which knowledge is evenly distributed, and learners acquire abilities and knowledge that have positive impacts on society. This strategy is performed best when applied to collaborative projects. It begins by urging the student to concentrate on what is right instead of wrong.

The more modern humanist theories, or pluralistic approaches, take into consideration how, in contemporary culture, historically polarized notions of right and wrong have disintegrated into facts. This attitude reflects the emphasis placed on embracing diversity in many institutions and societies.

These humanistic learning techniques all place a strong focus on active learning. Also, there are two variations of the humanistic approach. The simplest form of learning is the transmission of knowledge or pedagogy. The terms *andragogy* and *pedagogy* highlight the distinction between earlier training models and today's more prevalent method. But andragogy adds appeal by giving the student complete control over their education.

Any ability can be taught using the humanistic approach; its only distinction is that the learner is mainly in charge, which is why this method works for people who are highly motivated to learn. It's best for group-based or spiritual learning. With this method, you can learn anything—from cooking to computing to calligraphy—as long as you're willing to take action and be accountable!

PEDAGOGY

Pedagogy is primarily centered on instruction. Knowledge

is formally conveyed from someone who has it to someone who does not. This kind of model has often been used in institutional settings, such as schools and other places of higher learning, where it may be administratively simpler to assume control of the learning experience while neglecting the abilities or needs of the individual to engage in conscious learning. Unfortunately, this model has the potential to inspire hostility or rebellion, especially in older kids, teenagers, and adults.

It could be argued that pedagogy misses the point because giving instruction or training does not guarantee that the recipient will like it, remember it, or even be able to apply it in practical situations.

ANDRAGOGY

Andragogy offers a process in which the learner, assisted by a supervisor, perhaps a coach or mentor, acquires knowledge at a pace that suits them. There are four foundations of the andragogical theory, distinguishing it from pedagogy and other conventional learning techniques.

- The freedom to develop one's learning is necessary for the learner.
- For understanding and new learning to happen appropriately, the learner's prior experiences are essential.
- Instead of being driven by fear or coercion, the person needs to be open to learning.
- The importance of the learning orientation, which is learner-centered rather than subject-oriented, cannot be overstated.

Establishing a supportive and welcoming group atmosphere is crucial in the andragogy theory, as is informal individual assistance. Sharing experiences can enhance individual learning for both affective and cognitive processes. Participatory techniques build on personal and group experiences, promoting self-awareness, analysis, and attention-span extension.

OTHER APPROACHES TO LEARNING

Besides the main learning approaches we have discussed in this chapter, there are a few other approaches that can also be helpful for the learner. Let's briefly discuss them.

SOCIAL LEARNING

Social learning theory is the idea that learning is the direct result of interacting with the environment. According to Albert Bandura, people learn primarily through observation and modeling. Social learning and the behavioristic approach are closely related. In reality, it is a development of the same idea. Instead of concentrating on the learner's behavior, the social learning strategy entails observing the behaviors of others. Children, for instance, often imitate what they observe their parents doing. This method also highlights the idea that kids learn best by doing, regardless of their age or surroundings. There are many situations in life where interacting with others is necessary. Any skill that falls under this category is best learned through social learning. Social learning is a fantastic alternative if you want to master PR management approaches or marketing strategies. Similarly, this strategy effectively develops the ability to manage customer services.

Some of the subliminal principles of peer pressure are included in this theory. Pupils specifically watch other students and then model the appropriate behavior. Some people do it to look like their peers, and others do it to stand out. Gaining students' attention, emphasizing how they can remember information, establishing whether it's okay to repeat a previous activity, and ascertaining students' motivations are all necessary to utilize this approach.

CONSTRUCTIVE APPROACH

Ernst von Glasersfeld introduced the idea of constructivism, which holds that all knowledge is produced rather than acquired through the senses. Learners build new knowledge on the basis of previous knowledge. The constructivist learning approach is focused on building foundational knowledge. This method encourages practicing skills that demand the learner to be creative. Reflection and reevaluation are given a lot of attention in this technique. Forging associations and connections between new information and old knowledge will enhance the exploration tendencies in the mind of a learner. The constructivist learning approach is helpful for creative skills like directing a film or writing a play because it puts the learner in control of the learning direction.

The learner "constructs" a new understanding by drawing on prior knowledge and experience. Psychology argues that constructivism holds that learners can only create meaning by active engagement with the outside world, in contrast to the passive perspective of teaching that sees the learner as "an empty vessel" to be filled with knowledge.

EXPERIENTIAL APPROACH

David Kolb developed the experiential learning theory, which is an active learning process where students "learn by doing" and by reflecting on the experience. This theory is influenced by the works of John Dewey, Kurt Lewin, and Jean Piaget.

The experiential learning method is when you learn something by really doing it. Different types of encounters can teach you different things. This could involve observing an event, taking part in an event, deliberately trying out a new technique, or thinking back on any of these experiences. Regardless of the encounter, the learner must play a significant role in the incident. This results in first-hand education. This learning strategy should be used to tackle anything that calls for a practical perspective. This approach is therefore necessary for activities like swimming or playing any sport. You won't succeed even if you pay attention to and memorize all the instructions. You must go into the field.

This approach became an official learning theory in the early 1980s. It strongly emphasizes learning about something and then experiencing it, allowing students to apply their knowledge in practical settings.

CONNECTIVIST APPROACH

Two theorists named George Siemens and Stephen Downes initially proposed connectivism in 2005. Connectivism, influenced by the digital age, differs from constructivism by recognizing and filling in knowledge gaps. Connectivism, which is heavily impacted by technology, emphasizes a learner's capacity to regularly source and update accurate knowledge. Capacity is as crucial as knowledge to understanding where and how to look for it. Technology is accessible to almost everyone; thus, it becomes easy to update yourself on any hot topic.

Adult learners can significantly benefit from this theory. It suggests that new learning can effectively alter your world-view when your life experience, knowledge, and critical thinking combine. It is based on the transformation that occurs in your mind as you become an adult and start to analyze things on your own, instead of only using what people tell you.

People observe their surroundings and the rapid advancement of the world around them, feeling that their minds are transforming while unconsciously learning from their surroundings. These include religious beliefs and sometimes other societal constraints that they consider unnecessary as they grow up.

MEANINGFUL LEARNING APPROACH

The American psychologist David Ausubel created the meaningful learning theory. According to this hypothesis, a person's brain connects new knowledge with knowledge they already have. Contrary to memory or rote learning, in which you memorize concepts without the need to understand them, meaningful learning is based on acquiring quality learning and understanding concepts.

MULTIPLE INTELLIGENCE APPROACH

The American psychologist Howard Gardner is the one who came up with this notion. According to Gardner, each person has eight different bits of intelligence. This development relies on the individual's exposure to culture and environment. Gardner contends that not everyone learns in the same way, and that personalized and pluralized information enhances learning.

WHAT IS THE SIGNIFICANCE OF LEARNING THEORIES?

Humans have a natural need for knowledge. As a result, researching in the field of learning theories has become a career for many academics, philosophers, and opinion makers. The first step in improving learning is understanding how individuals learn.

After thorough research, researchers developed learning theories that explain how individuals learn. The understanding of how people learn and gain knowledge is based on theories. It shows how to define, evaluate, and forecast the learning process. It provides a wealth of knowledge regarding the creation, conception, and transfer of learning. Because of this, teachers, colleges, and programs for aspiring educators devote a lot of time to teaching about human development and various learning theories. All educators must have a solid understanding of how people learn, especially how a child learns and grows intellectually, to be the most successful teachers possible.

No two kids learn in the same way or at the same rate, just as no two individuals are the same. To address the needs of the "whole kid," effective educators must be able to adjust and design teaching that matches the needs of each student. A first step in achieving this is having a solid understanding of various learning theories, which is another reason why excellent instructors devote their entire lives to mastering both the art and the science of teaching.

Most teachers prefer to adhere to one or more theories, even if they do so unintentionally. Endorsing a specific learning theory isn't necessarily required in most teaching professions. However, learning more about each theory can help you become more successful in your quest for knowledge, whether you're an emerging or established teacher, a student, a parent of a student, or a combination.

Learning theories help teachers comprehend how their pupils learn. Teachers can create more complete learning strategies and assist pupils in succeeding in school by utilizing various teaching techniques. All aspects of learning, including the creation of a curriculum for formal education and how individuals engage in self-learning, can be influenced by learning theories. Although understanding some major educational theories can help anyone learn more about themselves and maximize their learning capacity, they are particularly crucial for aspiring and practicing teachers.

Learning theories benefit students by encouraging them to think critically about the various phases of education and the learning process. These theories primarily present conceptual frameworks that explain how information, knowledge, and skills can be used. It explains the value of education in many spheres of life. The frameworks can be studied by learners following the specifications to choose the best instructional implementations.

Learning theories come in various forms, so it is impossible to single out one as the greatest. Because each hypothesis has something unique to give, each theory illustrates a distinctive way to view learning and the key components that make it up. By employing specific learning theories as lenses, learning designers can comprehend the roles of a student and an instructor or facilitator. These beliefs have affected and molded teaching strategies and practices over time. A 2006 study found that learning theories are an incredibly important component of instruction. They support motivation and teaching strategies and offer learning environments. The teachers should first decide on their goals before selecting the appropriate theoretical framework because it includes a variety of facts and presumptions.

HOW EDUCATIONAL THEORIES INFLUENCE LEARNING

We have covered a wide range of learning theories, but do these ideas impact the learning process? Yes, of course. Not only that, but as time goes on, these theories get more advanced and practical. Different educational ideas have an impact on learning. Examples from learning theories can influence a teacher's approach to teaching and management. Finding the proper strategy can be the difference between an effective and exciting learning environment, even if it involves combining two or more learning theories.

The following are some of the ways that applied learning theories have an immediate impact on a learning environment:

- They provide a safe, stable atmosphere for the learner.
- They assist in aligning objectives among learners and their mentors.
- They give the freedom to make decisions about how to conduct practice sessions in manners that will best match the perceived requirements.
- They affect how and what a person learns.

- They assist third parties in figuring out the type of education a person has or is receiving to enhance their skill set.
- They help decide whether mentor-led or learner-led instruction will predominate.
- They help estimate the degree of collaboration that will occur in a learning environment.

HOW TO APPLY LEARNING THEORIES

The types of work environments one likes as an adult is influenced by the learning theories they encounter as a student. For instance, if someone had classes that primarily relied on social learning, they might be at ease in a collaborative work environment as adults. When viewing your fulfillment in a job as an adult, your educational background might be a helpful lens to use.

Since the time of Socrates, as well as the early proponents of behaviorism and cognitivism, educational theories have advanced significantly. Teachers and students can benefit from this growth as we continue to enhance our understanding of how people learn most effectively. Learning theories will undoubtedly continue to advance, and they will alter themselves according to the requirements of the time. This shows how significant and flexible these theories are.

The only approach to applying these concepts to real situations is fully comprehending them. Not all people respond favorably to the same approach, so just because one strategy works for someone else doesn't mean it will work for you too. Your awareness of your surroundings and yourself will help you understand what approach will work best for you. Therefore, selecting the learning strategy that will boost your productivity and learning speed is best.

CONCLUSION

You might not have been aware of the concept of rapid learning when you began reading this book. You could have been one of those people who believed that learning is a time-consuming, laborious process. Most people have this same perspective. If you are among those who believed this, then you were already subject to several restrictions that either you or others had placed on you whenever you tried to learn anything. These restrictions may have been conscious, unconscious, or both. Perhaps you desired to acquire a new skill but were sure that you lacked the necessary aptitude. Perhaps you aspired to learn a new language or sport, but as you heard the widespread belief that brain function declines with age, you gave up. Your inner critic kept telling you that you lacked the necessary skills and couldn't possibly learn anything new or develop yourself at that time. Perhaps you believed that no matter how hard you tried, you would always forget things. You had this strange conviction that you would never be able to recall the names of the attendees at your next social gathering, or that you would always be the dull person giving a speech while reading it off a piece of paper.

If any of this applied to you, you have probably changed after reaching the end of this book. I hope you're prepared to say goodbye to the person you used to be. You have now introduced the new, limitless learner. You have learned a great deal of information and found many skills in this book, and you have disproved all your prior preconceptions about learning. Now that you know which areas to focus on when learning your primary skill, you can create a skill tree. You are now confident that despite being an adult, your mind can still absorb information and learn new skills. Your knowledge of numerous learning approaches has improved your ability to study, and as a result, your mind can take in ten times as much information and keep it for longer.

You've expanded your potential, and you're now a limitless individual. You have stopped thinking that there are things you cannot do or cannot be. There may be things you haven't done yet or things you've struggled with in the past, but the limitless you is aware that the past doesn't predict the future, and now you can do anything you wish. Your infinite self is aware that, contrary to what you may have previously believed, your brain is a potent weapon that can acquire nearly any skill if you put your mind to mastering what you want to learn. The limitless you also possesses a limitless drive. Thoughts of a more ambitious existence may have crossed your mind in the past, but you may not have been able to motivate yourself to act upon them. But now that you understand how to match your habits with your goals, you can commit to lifelong learning.

You also understand how to take care of your mental

health by getting enough food, being in a positive environment, getting rest, and exercising so that you can tackle complex tasks whenever they arise. And you understand how to get in the flow so that, once you begin a task, you can fully immerse yourself in it. The ability to learn has been opened by the infinite you, which is probably the most significant development. You have significantly increased your learning power as a result of learning this. Besides a few physical restrictions, you can learn and accomplish anything. And you can learn anything faster now that you have the tools you need. Now that you've combined that with the knowledge you've received about remembering, thinking, reading, and expanding your attention, you have the magic wand that enables you to do almost anything.

I hope you use the knowledge you've learned from this book to enrich your life and the lives of those around you. You can also show your coworkers and friends how they might evolve into lifelong learners. They can take in information, retain it, and use it when necessary. Since this book also discusses how to discover your hidden talents, you'll be able to assist others in doing the same. Show them how to listen to their inner voice to attain inner peace and make a constructive contribution to society. Refer them to this book so they can also benefit from it and experience their superpowers.

I hope this book has equipped you with the knowledge necessary to learn complex skills. You don't have to be brilliant or exceptionally talented. To become extraordinarily productive, you only need to adhere to a few simple rules and create an appropriate schedule. You don't have to give up your job or pack up everything and relocate to another continent. You do not need to put your family aside. You can begin learning intelligently with proper time management and honest efforts toward your goal, with little to no time wasted on distractions.

I wasn't born with the ability to learn well or with a genius mind. I spent many years working on myself to master all these things, and I've tried to make it easier for you to get the most out of these skills. My learning process is still ongoing. Every day, I get new knowledge and comprehend a new learning strategy. Skills that were initially a complete mystery became understandable when I started practicing, and now I have mastered many skills that once felt impossible to learn. I only needed research and a few hours of regular, purposeful practice. These abilities are now a part of my life. It is simple to keep moving forward when the most crucial subskills are learned first. I'll be even better at each of these by the time you read this book. How much practice I put in will determine how much better I get. And you must also practice if you want to learn a new skill. There is no other option.

You can remove obstacles and change your surroundings to make practicing more manageable. You can develop clever techniques to enhance the effectiveness of your profession. But ultimately, you need to practice. The route that appears won't be that long and tiring if you put in sincere efforts. There are no shortcuts with zero practice—no training, then no skill development. That's how straightforward it is. The biggest obstacle to picking up new skills quickly isn't mental or physical; it's emotional. Trying something new at first is never comfortable, and it's easy to spend a lot of time and effort worrying about practicing rather than practicing.

You will always notice significant growth in the first ten to twenty hours of practice by scheduling time for it, conducting some preliminary research, and fighting against the initial discomfort. A period of effort, tenacity, and a little grit are all required to reap the benefits. Just pick one skill to learn. You don't need to choose several at a time. Make a commitment to trying a skill on your to-do list. Play a particular instrument, learn a sport, work on a task, learn a language, prepare a meal, or draw some art. It feels challenging, but it is not.

One more thing: Today is the only day you have the freedom to choose to practice. Not the next day, not next week, not in a month, and not a year from now. Only today. You have a decision to make when you wake up. You can decide to devote your time to learning skills that will improve your success, pleasure, and life rewards. Alternatively, you can waste yourself by wasting your precious time.

You have discovered the little-known techniques for carrying out everything on these pages. You know how your brain works and how to prepare it for learning. You are aware of the strategies to maintain its interest. Now that you have access to the same time-tested memory strategies that world record holders utilize, you can unleash the extraordinary power of your memory. You also have a method in place for preserving your memories over time. This foundation will save countless hours no matter what you choose to learn. But learning is much more than just recalling information and reviewing it.

Fortunately, you can thoroughly research any subject to develop the best action plan. You have the ability to pre-read and critically evaluate any material you choose to study. With sufficient effort, you may double or triple your reading speed while retaining a high level of comprehension. As you move on to study the subsequent subject that piques your interest, you'll be stunned by the strength of these ostensibly simple skills. If you develop engaging ways to gauge your learning and impart knowledge to others, you can learn even the most challenging concepts rapidly. You currently know a great deal more than those around you.

You've come to the conclusion that you truly are a super learner. The most valuable skills I can teach someone are included in this book. They are some of the greatest things I have ever been given, and they are now at your disposal; benefit from them, take pleasure in them, and better yourself. I hope that all you have learned will prove fruitful to you in life, in whatever field you wish to pursue.

REFERENCES

First Chapter

[1] Schilling, D. R. (2017, June 13). *Knowledge doubling every 12 months, soon to be every 12 hours*. Industry Tap. https://www.industrytap.com/knowl edge-doubling-every-12-months-soon-to-be-every-12-hours/3950

[2] Toker, Daniel, and Friedrich T. Sommer. "Information Integration in Large Brain Networks." *PLOS Computational Biology*, vol. 15, no. 2, 7 Feb. 2019, p. e1006807, 10.1371/journal.pcbi.1006807.

[3] Cabib, S., Campus, P., Conversi, D., Orsini, C., & Puglisi-Allegra, S. (2020). Functional and Dysfunctional Neuroplasticity in Learning to Cope with Stress. *Brain Sciences*, *10*(2), 127. https://doi.org/10.3390/brain-sci10020127

[4] Engen, T. (1991). Odor Sensation and Memory. In *Google Books*. Greenwood Publishing Group. https://books.google.com.pk/books?id=4c8zvctk YuwC&dq=sense+of+smell+related+to+memory&lr=&source= gbs_navlinks_s

[5] Jonassen, D. H., & Driscoll, M. P. (2004). *Handbook of Research for Educational Communications and Technology : a Project of the Association for Educational Communications and Technology*. Hoboken: Lawrence Erlbaum Associates.

[6] *Talents*. (n.d.). Dota 2 Wiki. Retrieved August 18, 2022, from https://dota2. fandom.com/wiki/Talents

[7] SHULMAN, L. S. (1986). Those Who Understand: Knowledge Growth in Teaching. *Educational Researcher*, *15*(2), 4–14. https://doi.org/10.3102/ 0013189x015002004

Second Chapter

[8] Potter, V. R. (1970). Bioethics, the Science of Survival. *Perspectives in Biology and Medicine*, *14*(1), 127–153. https://doi.org/10.1353/pbm.1970.0015

Third Chapter

[9] Meadows, M. (2015). Confidence: How to Overcome Your Limiting Beliefs

and Achieve Your Goals. In *Google Books*. Meadows Publishing. Retrieved from https://books.google.com.pk/books?hl=en&lr=&id=9yzaBw-AAQBAJ&oi=fnd&pg=PT4&dq=Limiting+beliefs+frequent-ly+emerge+in+our+self-talk

[10] Drewery, D. W., Sproule, R., & Pretti, T. J. (2020). Lifelong learning mindset and career success: evidence from the field of accounting and finance. *Higher Education, Skills and Work-Based Learning, 10*(3), 567–580. https://doi.org/10.1108/heswbl-03-2019-0041

[11] Radford, B. (1999). *The Ten-Percent Myth*. Retrieved from https://cdn.centerforinquiry.org/wp-content/uploads/sites/29/1999/03/22164948/p52.pdf

[12] Dilmurod, R., Akmal, A., & Dostonjon, R. (2020). Research On Effective Ways To Intelligence Quotient Of Perception Through Mobile Games. *The American Journal of Applied Sciences, 02*(08), 89–95. https://doi.org/10.37547/tajas/volume02issue08-12

Fourth Chapter

[13] Hadavi, S. (2017). Direct and Indirect Effects of the Physical Aspects of the Environment on Mental Well-Being. Environment and Behavior, 49(10), 1071–1104. https://doi.org/10.1177/0013916516679876

[14] Lugavere, M., & Grewal, P. (2021). Genius Food: Become Smarter, Happier, and more productive while protecting your brain for life. Harper Wave.

[15] da Mota Gomes, M. (2020). Unveiling sleep mysteries: functions. Revista Brasileira de Neurologia, 56(1).

[16] Wood, W., Quinn, J., & Kashy, D. (2002). Habits in Everyday Life: Thought, Emotion, and Action. Journal of Personality and Social Psychology, 83(6). https://doi.org/10.1037/0022-3514.83.6.1281

[17] Cunningham, A. E., & Stanovich, K. E. (1998). What reading does for the mind. American educator, 22, 8-17.

Fifth Chapter

[18] Mohan, A., Sharma, R., & Bijlani, R. L. (2011). Effect of Meditation on Stress-Induced Changes in Cognitive Functions. *The Journal of Alternative and Complementary Medicine*, *17*(3), 207–212. https://doi.org/10.1089/acm.2010.0142

[19] Fuller, J. R. (1988b). Martial arts and psychological health. *British Journal of Medical Psychology*, *61*(4), 317–328. https://doi.org/10.1111/j.2044-8341.1988.tb02794.x

[20] Sharma, M. (2013). Yoga as an Alternative and Complementary Approach for Stress Management. *Journal of Evidence-Based Complementary & Alternative Medicine*, *19*(1), 59–67. https://doi.org/10.1177/2156587213503344

[21] Okano, K., Kaczmarzyk, J. R., Dave, N., Gabrieli, J. D. E., & Grossman, J. C. (2019). Sleep quality, duration, and consistency are associated with better academic performance in college students. *Npj Science of Learning*, *4*(1). https://doi.org/10.1038/s41539-019-0055-z

[22] Davies, M. A. (2000). Learning ... the Beat Goes on. *Childhood Education*, *76*(3), 148–153. https://doi.org/10.1080/00094056.2000.10522096

Sixth Chapter

[23] Lee, T. D., Swanson, L. R., & Hall, A. L. (1991). What Is Repeated in a Repetition? Effects of Practice Conditions on Motor Skill Acquisition. *Physical Therapy*, *71*(2), 150–156. https://doi.org/10.1093/ptj/71.2.150

[24] Hodges, N. J., & Williams, A. M. (2012). Skill Acquisition in Sport: Research, Theory and Practice. In *Google Books*. Routledge. https://books.google.com.pk/books?hl=en&lr=&id=03BZqb9kR90C&oi=fnd&pg=PP2&dq=practice+and+skill+acquisition&ots=u2piaNM3Su&sig=FsPCYroBI-y5FXo7__k5RlWiZwY&redir_esc=y#v=onepage&q=practice%20and%20skill%20acquisition&f=false

Seventh Chapter

[25] Bucciarelli, M. (2007). How the construction of mental models improves learning. *Mind & Society*, *6*(1), 67–89. https://doi.org/10.1007/s11299-006-0026-y

[26] Mendoza, J. S., Pody, B. C., Lee, S., Kim, M., & McDonough, I. M. (2018). The effect of cellphones on attention and learning: The influences of time, distraction, and nomophobia. *Computers in Human Behavior*, *86*, 52–60. https://doi.org/10.1016/j.chb.2018.04.027

Eighth Chapter

[27] Wei, Y., Shi, Y., MacLeod, J., & Yang, H. H. (2022). Exploring the Factors That Influence College Students' Academic Self-Efficacy in Blended Learning: A Study From the Personal, Interpersonal, and Environmental Perspectives. *SAGE Open*, *12*(2), 215824402211048. https://doi.org/10.1177/21582440221104815

[28]Vanderstraeten, R., & Biesta, G. (1998). Constructivism, Educational Research, and John Dewey. *The Paideia Archive: Twentieth World Congress of Philosophy*, 34–39. https://doi.org/10.5840/wcp20-paideia1998235

[29] Khatib, M., Sarem, S. N., & Hamidi, H. (2013). Humanistic Education: Concerns, Implications and Applications. *Journal of Language Teaching and Research*, *4*(1). https://www.academia.edu/36137072/Humanistic_Education_Concerns_Implications_and_Applications?auto=citations&from=cover_page

[30] Bremser, W. G., & White, L. F. (2000). An experiential approach to learning about the balanced scorecard. *Journal of Accounting Education*, *18*(3), 241–255. https://doi.org/10.1016/s0748-5751(00)00016-6

[31] Silva, J. B. da. (2020). David Ausubel's Theory of Meaningful Learning: an analysis of the necessary conditions. *Research, Society and Development*, *9*(4), 3. https://dialnet.unirioja.es/servlet/articulo?codigo=7423145

[32] Morgan, H. (1996). An analysis of gardner's theory of multiple intelligence. *Roeper Review*, *18*(4), 263–269. https://doi.org/10.1080/02783199609553756

[33] Wilson, S., & Peterson, P. (2006b). *Theories of Learning and Teaching What Do They Mean for Educators?* https://files.eric.ed.gov/fulltext/ED495823.pdf

THANK YOU

As a way of saying thank you for purchasing this book and making it all the way until the end, I would like to give you free access to the **Mastering Personal Growth Starter Kit**.

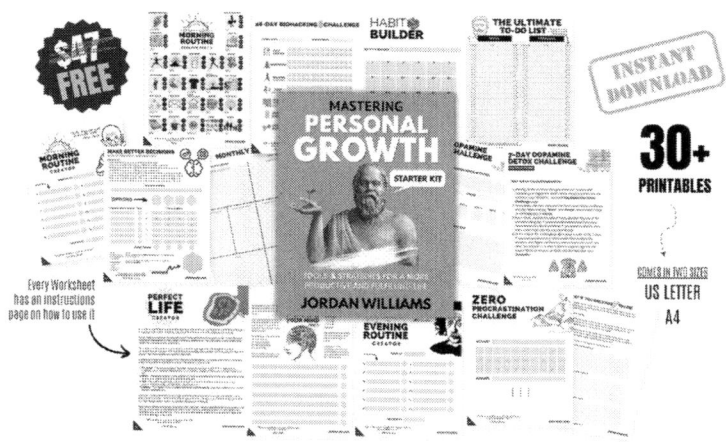

Inside you'll find <u>over 30 printables</u> designed to help you create a more productive and fulfilling life.

You'll get practical tools for:

- developing good habits
- making better decisions
- organizing your everyday tasks

- eliminating procrastination
- biohacking for ultimate performance and wellbeing
- finding your passions
- creating your perfect life
- boosting your self-esteem
- creating powerful daily routines
- and much more!

It's always possible to take control of your life and start living with intention - so why wait? Get the **Mastering Personal Growth Starter Kit** now and take the first step towards a better future.

Just go to jordanwilliamsofficial.com or scan the QR code below:

One more quick thing before you go!

If you had a great time reading this book, it would mean the world to me if you could leave a review on Amazon.com.

Reviews really help authors like me, and it would be incredible to hear your honest thoughts and feedback about the book. Plus, it helps other readers like you find the book and make a more informed decision about whether this book is right for them.

So, if you have a minute to spare, I would appreciate it if you could leave a review. Again, thank you so much for your time, and I wish you all the best on your journey to personal growth and self-mastery.

ABOUT THE AUTHOR

Jordan Williams is an author in the field of personal growth who is dedicated to helping people reach their full potential and live a happier, healthier, wealthier, and more fulfilling life. Through his work, Jordan has made it his mission to empower individuals to become the best version of themselves by teaching them how to think better, learn new skills faster, reach their goals, and become more productive. With his guidance, Jordan has demonstrated time and time again that anyone can make great strides in improving their lives and reaching their personal goals. His knowledge and expertise in this field have provided readers with valuable insight and resources for them to take their lives to the next level.

facebook.com/jordanwilliamsofficial

youtube.com/@jordan_williams

tiktok.com/@jwilliams_official

pinterest.com/jordanwilliamsofficial

Made in the USA
Columbia, SC
17 March 2024

33190993R00114